ORGANIZATION SIZE, JOB SATISFACTION, ABSENTEEISM AND TURNOVER

Kenneth A. Kovach

E 70

University Press of America

Copyright © 1978 by

University Press of America, Inc.™

4710 Auth Place, S.E., Washington, D.C. 20023

All rights reserved

Printed in the United States of America

ISBN: 0-8191-0242-3

658.314
K88

TABLE OF CONTENTS

Chapter		Page
I.	INTRODUCTION	1
II.	REVIEW OF LITERATURE	17
III.	METHODOLOGY	48
IV.	STATISTICAL ANALYSIS AND FINDINGS	61
V.	CONCLUSIONS AND IMPLICATIONS	86
APPENDIX A		100
APPENDIX B		114
SELECTED BIBLIOGRAPHY		145
AUTHOR'S INDEX		152

LIST OF TABLES

Table		Page
I.	Table 4.1: Catagorization of Subjects	62
II.	Table 4.2: Absenteeism Index	64
III.	Table 4.3: Turnover in Field	65
IV.	Table 4.4: Turnover in Organization	66
V.	Table 4.5: Stability Rate	67
VI.	Table 4.6: Correlation Between Total Absence and Degree of Satisfaction From Various Sources: All Subjects	70
VII.	Table 4.7: Correlation Between Total Absence and Degree of Satisfaction From Various Sources:. 25 Day Cut-off	71
VIII.	Table 4.8: Satisfaction From Various Sources, Across Organization Size	73
IX.	Table 4.9: Same Line of Work if Relive Life	74
X.	Table 4.10: Correlation: Overall Satisfaction-Turnover, Stability	75
XI.	Table 4.11: Hourly Rate of Pay	76
XII.	Table 4.12: Benefits Offered	77
XIII.	Table 4.13: Individual Value Systems: Orientations Toward Work (All Responses)	80
XIV.	Table 4.14: Individual Value Systems: Orientations Toward Work (Without Promotions, Subordinates, Amount of Work)	81
XV.	Table 5.1: Partial Correlations	90

I INTRODUCTION

Statement of the Problem

The basic intent of this book is an empirical investigation of one aspect of what is commonly called the 'size-effect' in industrial organizations. As used here, the 'size-effect' refers to that condition observed by Ingham[1] whereby, as the size of an organization increases, worker's attachment to the organization, as measured by absenteeism, decreases; overall job satisfaction and its corollary, turnover, are unaffected. The difference in the results obtained between attachment, as measured by absenteeism, and overall satisfaction, as measured by turnover, is based on quality and quantity of job satisfaction. A feeling of attachment is a possible result of certain sources of satisfaction and, if Ingham is ocrrect, will be reflected in absenteeism rates. Turnover rates, on the other hand, will be a result of overall levels of job satisfaction, according to Ingham.

The problem dealt with here concerns the impact which organizations of various sizes have on quality and quantity of job satisfaction as manifested in absenteeism and/or turnover rates. Included is an investigation of the individual differences in subjects' reactions and subsequent responses to differences in organization size. The author believes that such differences center around the value systems of the subjects. Specifically, the 'orientation toward work' by the individual is a key variable. For present purposes 'orientation toward work' will be taken to mean the individual's attitudes toward work in general as well as specific aspects of that work, i.e., those factors he deems important and unimportant about a job and the things within the work environment that cause him to be satisfied or dissatisfied. Orientation toward work is thus that segment of the individual's value system of immediate concern here.

If the employee values such employment conditions as vertical participation in work related affairs, horizontal interaction with co-workers, and frequent contacts with superiors and subordinates, then we are likely to find a high degree of attachment to the organization if these conditions are met. Conversely, if he values monetary compensation to the degree that it dominates other considerations, we are not likely to find this attachment, even though his overall satisfaction level, assuming he perceives the monetary rewards as equitable, may be as high as the individual who is more concerned with the factors mentioned above. The author believes, and will attempt to show, that smaller organizations are more likely to offer these social[2] and task rewards, while larger organizations offer higher economic rewards.

An analysis of the individual sources of job satisfaction is thus needed to explain differences found in absenteeism across organization size, while overall levels of satisfaction should be related to turnover rates.

Thus the study will initially be descriptive in nature, comparing absenteeism and turnover rates of large and small organizations. This being accomplished, the nature of the relationship found between company size and turnover and absenteeism rates will be related to differences in levels of overall job satisfaction and to individual sources of satisfaction.

Additionally, a test will be made of the hypothesis that levels of job satisfaction are determined by the amount of congruence between individual value systems (here represented by the job components the subject indicates are most important) and organizational reward systems (whether economic, task, or social rewards are more available through the job).

The sample used for this study will consist of skilled and unskilled blue collar workers in the solid waste disposal industry of the United States.

Much has been written by social scientists about the internal changes that take place as an organization grows in terms of number of employees.[3] Changes in size seem to be associated with changes in such areas as productivity levels,[4] orientations toward work by individual members,[5] types of power bases used and perceived,[6] and leadership styles employed,[7] among others. A few previous studies have shown a direct or indirect connection between each of these variables and overall size on the one hand and job satisfaction on the other.[8] This particular study explores the association between size, and job satisfaction and its components or sources, as manifested in absenteeism and turnover rates. This area has been the focus of far fewer investigations than any of those mentioned above.

Many of the prior investigations done on the size-effect start with changes in overall number of employees and describe correlated changes in one or more of the above mentioned factors, including job satisfaction. This is fine as far as it goes, yet there is a need to deal with the question of causality as well as correlation, a question too often neglected in other studies.

Another common type of study starts with measured levels of job satisfaction and then attempts, through observation, to identify variables within the work environment contributing to observed levels.

In a few studies these variables are then related to organization size. While both this approach and the one mentioned above contribute to a better understanding of the human element in business and industrial organizations, it is more important to see the connection between the two. In other words, rather than on the one hand starting with changes in size and then observing other concurrent internal changes, and on the other hand starting with levels of job satisfaction and searching for contributory factors, an attempt should be made to directly associate factors of company size and employee satisfaction. Satisfaction levels should be contingent upon the congruence between individual value systems and conditions or factors resulting from changes in size.[9] It is such a relationship that the author examines in the present study.

Leaving aside temporarily questions of causality, it is the author's belief that there are important connections to be drawn between organization size and individual satisfaction and that these connections have intervening variables similar to those mentioned above, i.e., types of power used, orientations toward work, etc. Furthermore, a fact either unrecognized or unaccounted for by many writers is that given the same starting point in terms of size and the same set of variables, the resultant levels of job satisfaction among individuals may be significantly different due to variations in perceptions and value systems. This being the case, it is vital in a study of this type to use individual value systems as an explanatory variable when associating size and satisfaction.

The problem then is to find and explain connections between manifestations of job satisfaction, i.e., absenteeism and turnover, and organization size. To do this, a bridge of intervening variables must be built between the two as follows: reward systems emphasizing economic, task, or social aspects must be shown to be related to size, and the degree of congruence between individual value systems and these rewards must be correlated with levels of job satisfaction.

The Need for Such a Study

This study in many respects parallels the earlier work of Ingham[10] in England. Ingham found that as organization size increased, so did the level of "bureaucratization",[11] leading in turn to more specialization in areas of production and administration. As a firm grew in size, it was thus able to offer its employees fewer social and task rewards due to more hierarchical levels and a finer division of labor. As these types of rewards decreased in availability, economic rewards increased proportionately, due in part to economies of scale. Large firms, with their greater emphasis on economic rewards, were attractive to workers with corresponding value systems. Small firms, with their emphasis on social and task rewards, appealed to those with this value system. Ingham found that turnover was constant across organizations of different size because those with each type of value system were equally successful in choosing a firm with a congruent reward system. He also found that the higher level and the particular type of social rewards associated with smaller organizations led to a feeling of identification with the firm on the part of the individual. Such a feeling was not present in larger organizations where the rewards were more economic. This explained his finding that absenteeism rates were lower in the smaller firms than in the larger.

In light of Ingham's findings, a question may arise regarding the need for another study of this nature. Yet, it must be remembered that

Ingham's study used skilled and semi-skilled blue collar workers in the light engineering industry as subjects and was confined geographically to Bradford, England. As he himself points out, there has been no explanatory study of the size-absenteeism-turnover relationship in American industry.[12]

The author feels that the differences in social structures and technological states between the light engineering industry in Bradford and other types of industry, including solid waste management, in this country are of such a nature that they make questionable any assumed projection of Ingham's findings. Likewise, a study such as this across geographic regions discounts the possibility of contaminating variables unique to a particular area affecting the findings.

Despite the fact that other writers, in addition to Ingham, have dealt with specific aspects of this problem, it has yet to be satisfactorily approached in its entirety in this country. There are those such as Hewitt[13] who have looked at absenteeism and found it to be lower in smaller units than in larger and attributed this to lower satisfaction in the larger units. While this author accepts the data, he differs with its interpretation, and hypothesizes, based on the various studies of Goldthorpe[14] that it was quality of satisfaction as represented by commitment or attachment to the organization, and not quantity of overall job satisfaction that caused the difference in absenteeism rates. If Hewitt had included turnover in his study, he might have found similar rates across unit sizes and possibly concluded that quantity of satisfaction was, in fact, the same.

Cleland,[15] on the other hand, looks at turnover and neglects absenteeism. His belief is that labor turnover should be less in smaller plants due to the "intangible personal approach" used.[16] The author agrees that such an approach is to be found in small rather than large organizations. However, based on the work of Talacchi,[17] and Ingham,[18] this writer sees it as responsible for absenteeism, not turnover rates, and will investigate this relationship in the present study.

Others, such as Caplow,[19] concern themselves with the direct correlation between size and satisfaction. Caplow contends that organization size and employee satisfaction are not linearly related, but rather that certain increments of growth are more important than others for purposes of job satisfaction. Here again, this author considers this as investigation of only one aspect of the total problem, since no account is taken of individual differences. The same comment is applicable in regard to the work of Slater,[20] whose findings parallel those of Caplow in many respects.

As is shown in chapter II, several studies have dealt with intervening variables in the size-satisfaction relationship, such as structural levels, degree of participation allowed, leadership styles, etc. Here again, however, in most of these cases, no regard is given to differences between individuals and the value each places on the existence of such variables.

The point to be made here is that many researchers have dealt with one or more aspects of the 'size-effect' phenomena. The need still exists, however, to link the factors of organization size, reward systems, individual orientations to work, and resultant job satisfaction levels. The purpose of this book is to attempt to show one possible connection between these factors, using absenteeism and turnover data.

There is, in a broader sense, an additional need for studies of this type. Technological advances in this country since the Second

World War have caused production as a function of man hours to increase at something approaching a geometric rate. What this means is that more attention can be afforded the human element in the work place. Advances made by applied scientists must now be followed up by similar advances among those concerned with the social sciences. It is becoming increasingly important that we concern ourselves with this human element in the work place, and that we seek a new and better understanding of how best to handle it within the context of the many industrial changes brought about by technological advances. The technological advances themselves will continue to come, providing the proper economic climate exists. The question is, can social scientists give managers sufficient insight into the handling of individual employees as regards both their relations to each other and to the new technology.

It is important to recognize that in this country even those at the bottom of the wage structure are not forced to concern themselves solely with economic rewards to the extent that their very existence depends on them. This being the case, social/task rewards will become more important than in situations or locations where economic rewards are by necessity stressed more. What these social and task rewards are and the degree to which they are valued are, in a macro sense, a function of the nation's standards of living and, in a micro sense, a function of the individual's orientation toward work. At the level of the individual organization, it is the latter relationship which warrants study. If we are aware of the limitations imposed by size on the reward structure of the organization and, likewise, aware of the probably orientations toward work among employees in a given sized unit, we will have come a long way toward the ability to produce the desired congruence between individual values and organizational rewards. This book is intended to be a small step in that direction.

Methodology

A cross section of employees and organizations involved in solid waste management are used as subjects in this book.[21] For purposes of data collection organizations were randomly sampled, and were stratified along lines of geographic region, city size (based on the Standard Metropolitan Statistics Area System with cities randomly selected within each stratum), and whether they were publically or privately owned (with random sampling within each stratum for each city selected).

This sampling yielded 3,327 organizations, which were then asked to allow one management representative to be interviewed concerning management policies. Additionally, in approximately 30% of the organizations, permission was asked to conduct one employee interview. Stratifying variables in the employee sample were geographic region, public versus private ownership, and job level (managerial, clerical, supervisory/foreman, skilled labor, unskilled labor). Within each organization, the employee was chosen at random from the job category desired. The total sample size was in proportion to the estimated number of employees at each level in the total population.

In the present study, employees used as subjects are either skilled or unskilled blue collar workers.

Thus, responses to a previously administered structured interview are the source of data used.[22] Overall satisfaction levels are obtained indirectly through both a specific question addressing this point (If you had your life to live over, would you like to wind up in the same line of work as the one you're doing now?) and from responses indicating the individual's attitude toward specific sources or components of job satisfaction available in his particular firm. The sum of Likert Scale values for these components yield an additional measure of overall satisfaction. Satisfaction levels found across organizations of different sizes are compared within job levels. The size-satisfaction relationship found is then compared to turnover and absenteeism data gathered from the interview.

If, as the author originally suspected, satisfaction levels were found to be the same across organizations of various sizes, turnover should have also been the same, since it is viewed here as a manifestation of satisfaction.

If rates of absenteeism should differ across the size function, the sources of job satisfaction should be appropriate explanatory variables. Orientation toward work is determined from responses to questions concerning things on or about the job giving the most pleasure, the recollection of a particular incident leading to a feeling of satisfaction, and the individuals reason for choosing this line of work.

It is expected that the value system of those in small firms will place a greater emphasis on social and task rewards while those in large firms will be more inclined toward economic rewards. Thus, the sources of job satisfaction included in the interview were classified as either economic, task, or social and the author looks at the relationship between the sources, orientation toward work, and the size of the organization employing the respondent.

It is hypothesized that the nature of the social and task components will give rise to a greater "attachment or commitment to work" among those individuals who value such a reward system. It is only in smaller organizations, with their lesser amounts of 'bureaucratization' that a reward structure can be offered that emphasizes these social and task components. For this reason, the author compares absenteeism rates, viewed here as a manifestation of commitment to work, for different sized organizations, with the expectation that they will be smaller in smaller sized firms.

In summary then, this study looks at the relationship between organizations of various sizes and rates of absenteeism and turnover. The initial hypothesis is that differences in these two rates will be manifestations of different sources and levels of satisfaction between organizations.

Hypothesis

As should be evident by now, it is the opinion of the author that levels and sources of job satisfaction are reflected in rates of turnover and absenteeism, respectively.

Job satisfaction as used here is not to be confused with one of its possible sources, a feeling of 'closeness' to the organization by the individual. Satisfaction levels can have many sources or components, i.e., monetary compensation, security, interpersonal relations, etc. This closeness or 'attachment' to the organization may be one possible expression of job satisfaction. It represents (1) a feeling on the part of the individual that his goals and those of the organization can best be served together, (2) an identification with the organization and its members, and (3) a feeling of commitment to his job and his co-workers.

The author seriously doubts if this feeling of attachment is possible without a sense of job satisfaction by the individual, yet, likewise, feels that it is not a mandatory condition leading to satisfaction. It is one of the sources that could _possibly_ contribute to satisfaction; no single source is by itself a requirement.

It is hypothesized that overall satisfaction levels are the same in large and small organizations. This is felt to be true because job satisfaction is directly related to the degree of congruence between individual value systems and organizational reward systems. There is no reason to suspect that individuals with one set of values are any more accurate in their employment choices than those with another value system are in theirs. Since turnover is a manifestation of satisfaction, it will, therefore, be the same across different sized organizations, despite the fact that these organizations may offer different rewards.

Absenteeism, on the other hand, relates to the <u>sources</u> of job satisfaction. In those organizations where social and task rewards are more important, employees in general[23] will feel a greater sense of attachment and commitment to the job than will those in an organization that stresses economic rewards. Smaller firms are better able to offer these social and task rewards due to lower levels of bureaucratization. Since absenteeism is directly related to this feeling of commitment as a source of job satisfaction, it is hypothesized that rates of absenteeism will be lower in smaller organization.

To capsulize the main idea, then:

H_o: Quantity of Satisfaction   = Quantity of Satisfaction
         Larger Organizations   Smaller Organizations

Therefore:

H_o: Turnover   = Turnover
         Larger Organizations   Smaller Organizations

This is true despite this satisfaction coming from different sources, not the least important of which is a feeling of attachment to the organization. The presence or lack of satisfaction from this particular source leads to the following:

H_o: Qualtiy of ← − − − − different than → Quality of
      Satisfaction   Satisfaction
      (Sources)   (Sources)
      Larger   Smaller
      Organizations   Organizations

                Sources of Satisfaction
                Larger = Economic

      Sources of Satisfaction
        Smaller = Social and Task = Feelings of identity with and
                                                      commitment to the organization

Therefore:

H_o: Absenteeism   Absenteeism
      Larger Organizations   Smaller Organizations

due to the inverse relationship between organization size and individual attachment and the fact that smaller firms are better able to foster this feeling.

It is important to once again emphasize that this feeling of attachment to the organization is not a <u>necessary</u> source of job satisfaction, only a possible one. The existence of such a feeling is in large part dependent on an individual value system emphasizing social/task rewards and an organizational reward system offering them.

The author feels the need to make one final comment in the hope that it will serve as a transition from this introductory chapter to a review of the literature. The majority of recent studies concerning job satisfaction deal exclusively with social or non-economic rewards and their impact on job satisfaction. The author suspects that this is a result of the over zealous interpretation of the Hawthorne findings by many educators and researchers. While this is, indeed, a fruitful area of study, there appears to be an overemphasis in recent literature on the rewards of this nature. This imbalance is so great that one may well come away with the impression that all workers are satisfied by such rewards. Not nearly enough is being done in the area of monetary rewards and their effect on satisfaction levels. Those individuals whose value systems favor economic rewards are not being adequately dealt with in present social science literature, nor has the importance of these rewards been adequately acknowledged since the early findings of Argyle.[24] This book hopefully, will present a more balanced picture.

Footnotes

[1]Ingham, G. K., "Organization Size, Orientation to Work, and Industrial Behaviour", Sociology, Volume 1, 1967; Ingham, G. K., Size of Industrial Organization and Worker Behaviour, Cambridge University Press, 1970.

[2]As used here 'social' rewards do not include task rewards from the job, i.e., variety in the work, etc. The differentiation is between 'social', 'task', and 'economic' rewards.

[3]Hall, R. F., Hass, J. E., Johnson, N. H., "Organization Size Complexity, and Formalization", American Sociological Review, Volume 32, 1967; Filley, A. C., "A Theory of Small Business and Revisional Growth", Unpublished Ph.D. Dissertation, Department of Business Organization, Ohio State University, 1961; Caplow, T., "Organization Size", Administrative Science Quarterly, Volume 1, 1957; Cleland, S., The Influence of Plant Size on Industrial Relations, Princeton, 1955.

[4]Marriott, R., "Size of Work Group and Output", Occupational Psychology, Volume 26, 1949.

[5]Katzell, M. E., "Expectations and Dropouts in Schools of Nursing", Journal of Applied Psychology, Volume 52, 1968.

[6]Bachman, J. G., Smith, G. C.,Slesinger, J. A., "Control, Performance, and Satisfaction: An Analysis of Structural and Individual Effects", Journal of Personality and Social Psychology, Volume 4, 1966.

[7]Filley, A. C., and House, R. J., Managerial Process and Organizational Behavior, Glenview: Scott, Foresman, 1969.

[8]Beer, M., "Organizational Size and Job Satisfaction", Academy of Management Journal, Volume 7, 1964; Worthy, J., "Organizational Structure and Employee Morale", American Sociological Review, 1950.

[9]Hackman, J. R., and Lawler, E. E. III, "Employee Reactions to Job Characteristics", Journal of Applied Psychology, Volume 55, 1971; Macedonia, R. M., "Expectation-Press and Survival", Unpublished Doctoral Dissertation, Graduate School of Public Administration, New York University, June, 1969.

[10]Ingham, G. K., "Organization Size, Orientation to Work and Industrial Behaviour", Sociology, Volume 1, 1967; Ingham, G. K., Size of Industrial Organization and Worker Behaviour, Cambridge University Press, 1970.

[11]A greater division of labor, an increase in the number of structural levels, and a greater reliance on formal rules and written communication.

[12]Ingham, G. K., Size of Industrial Organization and Worker Behaviour, Cambridge University Press, 1970, pg. 150.

[13] Hewitt, D., Parfit, J., "A Note on Working Morale and Size of Group", Occupational Psychology, Volume 27, 1953.

[14] Goldthorpe, J. H., "Orientation to Work and Industrial Behavior: A Contribution to an Acton Approach in Industrial Sociology," Unpublished Paper, Cambridge, 1964; Goldthorpe, J. H., "Social Stratification in Industrial Society" in Paul Halmos (ed)., The Development of Industrial Society, Sociological Review Monographic, 1964, pp. 97-122; Goldthorpe, J. H., "Attitudes and Behavior of Car Assembly Workers: A Deviant Case and Theoretical Critique", British Journal of Sociology, Volume 17, 1966.

[15] Cleland, S., The Influence of Plant Size on Industrial Relations, Princeton, 1955.

[16] IBID. The data deals with incidents of labor conflict as measured by number of strikes, and does not address the question of turnover.

[17] Talacchi, S., "Organizational Size, Individual Attitudes, and Behavior: An Empirical Study," Administrative Science Quarterly, Volume 5, 1960.

[18] Ingham, G. K., "Organization Size, Orientation to Work, and Industrial Behaviour", Sociology, Volume 1, 1967; Ingham, G. K., Size of Industrial Organization and Worker Behaviour, Cambridge University Press, 1970.

[19] Caplow, T., "Organization Size", Administrative Science Quarterly, Volume 1, 1957.

[20] Slater, P. E., "Contrasting Correlates of Group Size", Sociometry, Volume 21, 1958.

[21] Data was previously gathered through a study supported by Contract Number 68-03-0041 between the Environmental Protection Agency (E.P.A.) and Applied Management Sciences (A.M.S.), Silver Spring, Maryland.

[22] The complete Interview and Coding Manual are presented in Appendices A and B.

[23] Only those employees with the appropriate value system will be satisfied with these social and task rewards, yet in total the number of satisfied and dissatisfied employees in a firm offering such rewards will be the same as the number of each in a firm offering economic rewards.

[24] Argyle, Michael, el. al., "Supervisory Methods Related to Productivity, Absenteeism, and Labor Turnover", Human Relations, Volume 11, 1958.

II REVIEW OF LITERATURE

Due to the limited amount of literature concerned with the direct relationship between organizational size, and turnover and absenteeism rates, a review of the literature in this area would certainly be quite small. As Porter and Steers[1] point out, there is presently only one empirical study in this area,[2] and the author of that study correctly states that no work has been done in this area in the United States.[3]

If the relationship between size and absenteeism and turnover is expanded so as to include the single intervening variable of job satisfaction, a much more extensive review is possible. If the scope is widened still further to include studies dealing with specific sources of job satisfaction, it is possible, depending on the particular studies chosen, to begin to understand both the actions and interactions of the main and any impinging environmental variables between size and the two above mentioned rates. Finally, for purposes of explaining the possible relationship between job satisfaction and the 'size-effect' discussed in the previous chapter, individual orientations toward work must be considered.

What follows is not to be construed as an exhaustive review, particularly as regards job satisfaction, as this literature is extremely voluminous. It is instead intended to be a discussion of representative studies in this area. While reviewing literature dealing with organization size the focus is on the following two areas; general findings regarding size, and individual differences in work orientations and their relation to size. The general findings include such things as organization structure, amount and sources of job satisfaction, withdrawal in the form of turnover and absenteeism, incidents of labor conflict (strikes, etc.), and fluctuations in performance levels.

This chapter, then, is structured as follows:

Organization Size

(A) General Findings

    (1) structure

    (2) labor conflict (strikes, etc.)

    (3) performance levels

    (4) satisfaction (quantity, quality, related to organization level)

    (5) withdrawal (through absenteeism and turnover)

(B) Individual Differences (regarding orientation toward work)

(A) General Findings

Structure

Among other things, size and the resulting organization structure appear to be determinants of the type of power and supervisory style used. Bachman, Smith, and Slesinger[4] measured satisfaction by asking salesmen one direct question about how satisfied they were with their relationship with the office manager, their immediate supervisor. Having collected this information, they, then, determined the type of power used by asking the salesmen a fixed alternative question concerning why they obeyed the office manager. The salesmen were given five choices corresponding to French and Raven's[5] five types of power.[6]

Higher levels of satisfaction were found where expert and/or referent power was used, with a decided drop to levels found under reward, legitimate, and coercive types. Secondly, it was noted that the former two types were found most often in smaller organizations while the latter three predominated in those of a larger size. This supports the author's belief that the type of power used is often a function of unit size. Worthy's[7] work shows that supervisors in small organizations interact more frequently, both formally and informally, with subordinates than do those in larger organizations. If the supervisor is knowledgable as regards the tasks performed, the more frequent formal interaction would give expert power bases more of a chance to be realized. The more frequent informal interactions would allow a better chance for referent power bases to exist.

A supervisor in a larger, more bureaucratic, organization, with its greater reliance on written communication and formalized policies and rules[8] may not have reason to, or be able to, interact with subordinates as much and may, thus, be forced to rely on legitimate and reward power to a greater extent. This would explain the findings of Bachman, et. al., regarding organization size and types of power.

For purposes of the present study, the conclusions of Worthy and Bachman, et. al., cause the author to hypothesize that satisfaction levels with supervisory relations will be higher in smaller organizations. Inherent in an employees satisfaction with his supervisor are his feelings regarding the type of power exercised by that supervisor. Thus, other aspects of supervision being equal, the author would expect to find, on balance, higher satisfaction levels toward supervisors among employees in organizations using the more 'employee acceptable' types, i.e., the expert and referent power bases found more often in smaller organizations.

Responses to an inquiry in the questionnaire regarding relations with the immediate supervisor[9] are expected to support this hypothesis.

Weber's[10] claim that larger, more bureaucratic organizations have a greater dependence on formal rules and procedures, and on written as opposed to verbal communication also has implications for the leadership style used. Previous research has shown that a democratic leadership style is less likely to exist where the above conditions are present.[11] Thus, a democratic style is more likely to be found in smaller organizations.

In support of this idea, House and Miner[12] have shown that spans of control and overall organization size are positively correlated, and that as span of control increases, the leader exhibits more structured, directive, and autocratic leadership behaviour. This is done mainly for purposes of coordination. It is only as span of control decreases, i.e., in smaller organizations, that leaders can afford to use a more democratic style.

These findings, coupled with those of Filley and House[13] that employees are more satisfied under a democratic than an autocratic supervisory style reaffirm the author's hypothesis that supervisory relations will be more of a source of satisfaction in smaller organizations than in larger.[14]

Goldthopre, et. al.,[15] in their study of assembly line workers in the auto industry, found that employee participation in work related affairs and amount of interaction with other members decrease as organization size increases. Gouldner[16] found much the same thing in his earlier work with gypsum miners. The lack of tightly defined 'spheres of competence'[17] in smaller organizations, made possible by more formal control of the work procedures, served to increase the individuals range of interactions and degree of participation.

Indik[18] found that larger organizations need more control and coordination and by necessity become more bureaucratic. As the degree of 'bureaucratization' increased, Indik found that employee participation decreased (correlation of $-.53$, $p < .01$, on a sample of 32 business firms and 28 voluntary organizations ranging in size from 15 to 2,983 members). This decrease in participation led to what Indik described as a reduced 'attraction' to the organization and its other members by the employees studied.

Fisher,[19] in his study of male graduates at Los Angeles City College found, among other things, that organization size was inversely related to interaction. Mayo and Lombard,[20] while studying aircraft workers, used factors almost identical to those later mentioned by Indik, and found that what they term a feeling of 'closeness' to other workers decreased as size increased, due to the lesser number of both horizontal and vertical interactions.

The author feels that while the terminology may be different among the aforementioned studies, the basic point remains the same--size increases lead to decreases in member participation and interaction. Additionally, it is the author's belief that amount of participation and interaction are possible social sources of satisfaction. Hellriegel and Slocum[21] note that member satisfaction is directly related to opportunity for participation in organizational processes (decision making, etc.) and fulfillment of affiliation needs. House and Miner[22] state that satisfaction is related to formal and informal contact with other members in both horizontal and vertical directions.

The conclusion the author draws from the combined findings of such writers as Goldthorpe[23], Mayo and Lombard,[24] and Hellriegel and Slocum[25] is that participation and interaction should be more evident as sources of satisfaction in smaller, rather than larger, organizations. This being the case, the author expects such feelings to be one factor influencing satisfaction levels with supervisors (participation), subordinates, and co-workers (interaction). Measured satisfaction levels from these three sources in the present study are, thus, expected to be higher in smaller organizations.

Labor Conflict

The author believes that while the lesser amount of participation evidenced in larger organizations is one cause of the lower identity with the organization experienced by its members, one effect of such a feeling will be an increase in the number of labor conflicts. Certainly, one of the most notable and easily identified types of labor conflict is the employee strike. Since the number of strikes is easily quantified and their identification is purely objective, this measure of labor conflict has been used more than any other by researchers.

Other factors being equal, the number of strikes occurring across industrial organizations may well be partially dependent upon the degree of employee identity and commitment to the organization and its members. Since this feeling of identity is less in larger, more bureaucratic organizations,[26] it should be in this sector that the greater number of strikes occur. Should this be the case, it would serve as a reaffirmation of the previously stated thesis regarding size and employee satisfaction from certain social sources.

To reiterate the present point, smaller sized organizations give members a greater opportunity to participate, which, in turn, increases satisfaction levels from specific social sources such as relations with supervisors, etc. This, in turn, leads to a greater identity with the organization and reduces the number of incidents of labor conflict.

If the above reasoning is correct, a review of the relevant literature should show researchers finding more incidents of labor conflict (strikes) as organization size increases.

This is exactly what Cleland[27] found in his study of eighty industrial plants in the Trenton, New Jersey area. His data on incidence of strikes showed a direct association between organization size and labor conflict. Cleland states that this shows a decrease in satisfaction levels as size increases. The author would point out that such a decrease will not necessarily be present in overall satisfaction, but rather in the level from particular social sources--an important distinction.

Revans[28], likewise, found a direct relationship between strike activity and size in the British coal mining industry. He draws conclusions similar to those of Cleland regarding the implication of these findings for satisfaction levels and the author would reiterate his earlier point concerning specific social sources, rather than overall satisfaction.

The research linking labor conflict and size, thus supports the connection between size and levels of satisfaction from certain social sources.

Performance Levels

Some previous researchers have taken a look at the relationship between performance levels and size. Taken as a whole, the evidence to date offers support both for and against a connection between these two variables. Some of the previous studies find no relationship, and among those that do, there is no consensus as to the positive or negative nature of the connection.

Stekler,[29] in his study of diverse business firms used various profit ratios as indicators of overall performance level and found no correlation between any of these and size.

More often than profit ratios, productivity per worker is used as an indicator of performance level. Marriott[30] used this measure in a study of two motor car factories, a work often cited as a prime example showing an inverse relationship between size and performance. Except in the largest units (over 5,000) Marriott found that as size increased, productivity decreased. Yet this author would mention that the individuals studied by Marriott were paid on group incentive plans, which tend to become less effective in terms of motivational value as membership increases.[31] This may be one factor accounting for the findings. Likewise, as Argyle[32] points out, Marriott's subjects were members of assembly lines, where production levels depend on the speed of the slowest worker. The larger the group, the greater the probability that he will be slower.

Revans is another who attempts to show a connection between size and productivity. Working within the British coal industry,[33] he found that output per man hour was highest in middle sized units and lowest in both smaller and larger. He reaches similar conclusions based on evidence collected from retail establishments in the gas industry,[34] and proposes a curvilinear relationship between size and productivity.

Herbst[35] uses sales per person as his measure of performance and also finds a curvilinear relationship between the two variables--but in the opposite direction of that found by Revans. Sales per person were lowest in the middle ranges of size and highest in larger and smaller organizations.

The studies of Herbst and Revans are typical of the majority of works in the area of size and performance in that they study similar variables and offer contradictory results. Even the often quoted review of Porter and Lawler[36] which, like Marriott's aforementioned study, concluded that there was an inverse relationship between the variables, is filled with enough exceptions to be the subject of individual interpretation.

Also to be remembered is the fact that none of the aforementioned works has taken technological levels into account. As size increases, it seems logical to expect technology and relevant automation to be more of a factor in the production process. This may well be a crucial factor when productivity per individual is considered. Economies of scale are another factor overlooked by those such as Stekler[37] who deals with profit ratios and other monetary considerations.

It is the author's opinion that while past studies have not proven that a link exists between size and performance, they conversely have not shown that one does _not_ exist. Rather, the results to date have been contradictory and, thus, inconclusive. A stand on either side of this issue requires individual value judgments regarding the relative merit of the studies. The author choses to confront the question by starting with the works of Locke[38] and Bowen and Siegel[39], showing that under the right conditions, i.e., a responsive reward system, performance can be a causal factor leading to job satisfaction, and not the result of such satisfaction.

If performance by individuals is inversely related to size up to a point[40] as Marriott[41] and Herbst[42] suggest, and performance is also a causal factor in satisfaction levels when congruent reward systems exist, as Locke[43] and Bowen and Siegel[44] suggest, then satisfaction and size may be inversely related. The author adheres to this hypothesis with one major qualification. It is not overall satisfaction levels that are expected to vary inversely with size, but rather satisfaction from certain task related sources. Performance level as used here refers only to task related aspects of the total job. Thus, when it is said to be a causal factor in satisfaction, the author understands this to mean satisfaction from task related sources only.

In this investigation, then, the work itself[45] is expected to be more of a source of satisfaction among employees in smaller organizations than in larger.

Satisfaction

A review of the findings in the area of job satisfaction is best begun by looking at Worthy's[46] study at Sears and Roebuck. Using an employee questionnaire designed to measure individual attitudes toward the company in general, immediate supervisors, management, fellow employees, and working conditions, he was able to determine levels of job satisfaction and some possible reasons for such levels. Grouping the responses by division, Worthy found that unit size was the most important determinant of satisfaction levels. Not only did the employee in smaller divisions have higher satisfaction levels but the division's social structure was simpler, there were less levels of management, less subdivisions of work, and friendlier and closer relations between workers and between management and workers. Worthy's conclusion is that job satisfaction is related to 'integration', which is negatively related to structural complexity, which is, in turn, positively related to organization size. Filley,[47] and Terrien and Mills[48] have similar findings working with many of the same sources of satisfaction.

One must look behind Worthy's findings, however, and be aware of the fact that the sources of his measured job satisfaction are all social or task oriented. The author believes that this is what accounts for the inverse relationship between size and satisfaction. Economic sources must also be considered before one can speak of overall satisfaction levels.

Findings similar to those of Worthy are evidenced in the work of Thomas and Fink[49] as regards the two areas of group cohesiveness and division of labor. These authors found that as size increases, there is a decreasing group cohesiveness, a development of cliques, and a greater division of labor. These first two factors tie in with Worthy's[50] 'relations with co-workers'. Because of the decrease in factors such as cohesiveness, etc., as size increases, it is expected that when employees are questioned on co-worker relations for the present study[51] the amount of satisfaction derived from social sources will be inversely related to organization size.

The third relationship uncovered by Thomas and Fink, that of an increasing division of labor with growth in size, concerns itself with a task source of satisfaction, and is supported by the work of Talacchi.[52] Talacchi found that size increases lead to 'functional specialization', i.e., a narrowing of the work content and responsibility of individual positions. The author feels that because of this greater division of labor and functional specialization, satisfaction with the work itself and the variety present in the job will be less in large organizations than in small.

Hewitt and Parfit[53] also center on co-workers when studying the influence of size. They look at a single factory having numerous separate rooms with various sized work groups in each. Even though the workers in each room were not jointly paid and did not engage in active cooperation of the same job, Hewitt and Parfit observed that they did tend to behave like members of a group with common interests if the rooms were small enough for each member to be "familiar" with the others, i.e., if a situation existed where there was frequent informal interaction between workers. Absence rates varied depending on the degree of such interaction and, in the authors' opinions, reflected lower morale as room size increased.

This author notes that Hewitt and Parfit's definition of morale is contingent upon the degree of interpersonal relations with co-workers. Thus, the lower absenteeism found in smaller rooms is not a reflection of overall 'morale' as the term is commonly defined but is rather a reflection of the satisfaction level from a specific social source. Decreasing size allowed more horizontal interaction outside formal structural channels, thus increasing satsifaction from relations with co-workers.

Again, it is observed that the increasing structural complexity necessitated by an increase in size, actually decreases employees satisfaction from a social source.

There is also evidence to indicate that the organizational level of the employees being studied will be a factor influencing both the overall level of job satisfaction and the particular sources of such satisfaction. In general, the evidence supports the hypothesis of increasing satisfaction at each higher level.[54] This hypothesis has been supported not only in the private sector, but the public sector[55] and the military[56] as well, an important consideration for the present work which looks at both private and public organizations.

The present study deals exclusively with skilled and unskilled blue collar workers and, thus, does not concern itself with distinctions between other levels. When the influence of level combined with size is studied, however, such research has definite application to the present work. Porter[57] has done such a study, and found that in smaller organizations, non-supervisory personnel expressed more positive reactions regarding the work itself and the variety in the work[58] than their counterparts in larger organizations. For supervisory personnel, the findings were reversed, i.e., those at a higher level expressed a greater amount of satisfaction with such factors in larger organizations. Beer[59] uses a questionnaire as a direct measure of job satisfaction from sources similar to Porter's and arrives at a similar conclusion--lower level employees deriving more satisfaction from task sources than upper level in small organizations, with the situation reversing as organization size increases. Beer attributes his findings regarding lower level employees not to size per se, but to restrictions placed on lower level jobs through division of labor as size increases.

Since the present study deals with lower level personnel in both large and small organizations, the author expects to find satisfaction from task sources to be higher in smaller organizations. Such a finding would be consistent with the aforementioned research.

Withdrawal

For purposes of the present study, physical withdrawal from the job can take one of two possible forms--absenteeism or resignation (turnover). A connection is hypothesized to exist between these two forms of withdrawal, and sources and levels of job satisfaction. The nature of this connection is detailed in the introductory chapter, and evidence is presented in this section to support the author's belief in such a connection.

For present purposes, it is, thus, necessary to integrate studies dealing with both job satisfaction and withdrawal. In the area of job satisfaction, Viteles[60] and Hinrichs[61] have two of the most concise review publications, although Locke[62] and the most recent work of Lawler[63] delve into greater depth.

Two of the older, yet more extensive reviews of the literature regarding turnover and absenteeism were done by Brayfield and Crockett[64] and Herzberg, Mausner, Peterson, and Capwell.[65] Both of these reviews concluded that there is a consistent relationship between dissatisfaction and absence and turnover rates. Vroom's[65] work reinforces this notion by concluding that there is a negative relationship between satisfaction and turnover. Taylor and Weiss[66] administered the Minnesota satisfaction questionnaire to 475 employees of a discount store. Following up, one year later, they found that 'leavers' were significantly less satisfied than 'stayers' on 10 or 27 M.S.Q. scales. Their findings were, then, cross validated with another group of subjects. Here again, another piece of research seems to indicate that satisfaction levels and turnover are inversely related.[68]

Hulin[69] made use of the Job Description Index, developed by a group of researchers at Cornell University, to measure satisfaction levels of female clerical workers. Again, turnover was found to be negatively related to satisfaction levels. Waters and Roach[70] also looked at clerical workers and, using the same index, arrived at the same conclusion as Hulin.

Weitz and Nuckols,[71] working with life insurance agents, and Mikes and Hulin,[72] studying male and female office workers, arrived at a similar conclusion. Wild,[73] in his study of female operatives, presents some of the strongest statistical evidence in support of this point.

As the aforementioned studies are only representative of the many which reaffirm the inverse satisfaction-turnover relationship, the author feels safe in hypothesizing that such a connection will be found in the present study. Using this reasoning as a base, then, it seems reasonable to assume that the relationship found in the present study between job satisfaction and organization size will be reflected in an identical relationship between organization size and turnover.[74]

It is important to remember that the job satisfaction spoken of in the previous studies is <u>overall</u> job satisfaction, as opposed to satisfaction from specific sources. One of the two keys to this book is the author's hypothesis that overall satisfaction level will be the same across organizations of various sizes. This is so despite the fact that the amount derived from specific sources will vary with organization size. The author does feel that turnover is dependent on overall satisfaction levels and cannot be related to individual sources as some writers have tried to do, i.e., Ford[75] with job enlargement and Poidevin[76] and Kerr[77] with wages to mention only a few.

The other form of withdrawal, absenteeism, on the other hand, does have a dependence upon sources of job satisfaction. There are a number of studies showing the positive relationship of unit size and absenteeism. The present study concerns itself with non-supervisory workers, and using this sector of various organizations, researchers such as Kerr, Koppelmeier, and Sullivan,[78] Metzner and Mann,[79] Acton Society Trust,[80] and Baumagartel and Sobol[81] have all shown the positive nature of the size-absenteeism relationship. Statistically speaking, Indik[82] and Hewitt and Parfit[83] have offered the most conclusive evidence in this regard. Hewitt and Parfit studied factory workers working in different sized rooms and found absenteeism in small rooms to be less than one half of the standard for the factory as a whole. Absenteeism was nearly three times as common in medium size rooms and four times as common in large rooms as it was in small. Their findings are representative of those arrived at by researchers in this area.

Based on the volume of evidence presented, there seems to be little doubt concerning the nature of the size-absenteeism relationship.

The question now to be answered is, what is it about larger organizations that causes their employees to be absent more often?

To answer this question, one must begin by looking at the work of Talacchi[84] who used the Science Research Associates Employee Inventory over a five year period across 93 different companies, and concluded that there was an <u>inverse</u> relationship between organization size and job satisfaction from what he called the 'non-material'[85] sources. Waters and Roach[86] also found such a relationship between size and satisfaction from such non-material sources. Hewitt and Parfit[87] speak of 'lower morale' as organization size increases. The factors leading to this lower morale are supervisory and co-workers relations.

The non-material sources of Talacchi and Waters and Roach are similar to some of the 'social' sources used in the present study. The 'lower morale' spoken of by Hewitt and Parfit is a direct result of a decrease in satisfaction from certain social sources.

The General Electric Studies[88] of engineers, likewise, found employee satisfaction from a social source (supervisory relations) to be inversely related to absenteeism, although in this case size was not related.

Porter and Lawler's[89] review of the literature shows that increases in size decrease job satisfaction from social sources such as cohesiveness and communications, while Fisher,[90] and Mayo and Lombard[91] show that in such a situation feelings of attraction to the organization and closeness to fellow employees decreases.

Indik[92] and Thomas and Fink[93] show size increases to lead to greater task specialization and division of labor. From these latter two works, it appears that size increases adversely effect not only satisfaction from social sources, but task sources, i.e., the work itself and variety in the work, as well. Yet, the work of Porter and Lawler[94] shows that this is only the case at the non-managerial levels of the organization, and that as one moves up the hierarchy, this relationship changes. Porter and Lawler's findings are relevant for the present study, since the subjects used here are all located in the lower levels of the hierarchy.

It is possible to tie together the above studies by first restating the two main points they have made: (1) size is positively related to absenteeism and (2) size is inversely related to satisfaction from social and task sources at the lower structural levels.

This author, therefore, hypothesizes that, given the organizational level of the subjects interviewed for this book absenteeism will be determined by the amount of job satisfaction realized from social and task sources, and that this amount will be inversely related to organization size.

As regards turnover, it will be determined by the level of overall job satisfaction (from economic, as well as social and task sources). Although employees in large organizations are believed to derive more satisfaction from economic sources, while those in small are felt to realize more from social and task sources, the <u>overall</u> level is hypothesized to be the same across organization sizes.[95]

Before leaving the area the author wishes to offer an observation concerning previous studies regarding absenteeism and turnover and their relationship to satisfaction. In many of these earlier studies, little use has been made of cross organizational designs. Additionally, most use limited alternative questionnaires and, in the case of turnover, administer them to subjects who, if not already gone, are in the process of leaving. As will be shown in the following chapter, the present study differs in terms of methodology from those previously discussed.

(B) Individual Differences

There is little disagreement among researchers that, as in any large sector of the population, individual value systems are extremely heterogenous among industrial workers.[96] Yet, many of these same researchers who acknowledge such differences fail to account for them in their studies of job satisfaction. This is so despite the fact that the amount of job satisfaction experienced by any particular individual will be to a large extent dependent upon his value system. For purposes of the present study, the individuals 'orientation toward work', as defined in the Introduction will be that aspect of the total value system under consideration. There also appears to be considerable variation across individuals in this area. Miner[97] states that in his review of the research, the evidence clearly indicates that individuals' attitudes toward similar conditions within their work environments vary considerably. Ingham,[98] likewise, reviews the literature and determines that different individuals' orientations toward work can be classified as either economic or non-economic. Porter and Steers[99] state that individuals have different expectations concerning the work environment when they are hired, and that the variation in such expectations is the result of a similar variation in the individuals' attitude toward work.

The degree of which these individual value systems, as reflected in orientation toward work, are congruent with the reward system offered by the organization, appears to be the key to the level of job satisfaction. Locke[100] states, based on a literature review, that satisfaction is a function of value judgments made concerning the relationship between what is perceived to exist in the job situation and an individuals values and goals. Katzell,[101] and Porter and Steers,[102] feel that job satisfaction levels are a direct result of the discrepancy between the situations, rewards, and punishments an individual encounters on the job and what he expected, i.e., his 'met expectations'. Miner,[103] likewise, states that satisfaction with the job is dependent upon the closeness of the match between the individual's values and the organization rewards. Taken together, these studies indicate that serious problems will arise if individual differences are not taken into account.

One needs only to look at the contradictory nature of the findings when this factor is ignored to realize its importance. Farris[104] and Telly, et. al.[105] studied the effect of social aspects of the job on turnover and found a positive relationship, while others such as Taylor and Weiss[106] and Waters and Roach[107] looked at the same factors and found them to have a negative relation to turnover. Past literature contains numerous examples of such contradictory findings, and a failure to account for individual differences appears to be one reason.[108]

When one looks at those studies which have considered individual differences, it becomes apparent that value systems determine the level of employee satisfaction from all three source categories considered in this book.

As regards economic rewards, Locke, Bryan, and Kendall[109] found after five experiments that monetary incentives affected performance only through or by means of their effects on individuals goals or intentions. Schuster, Collette, and Knowles[110] found that equal increases in economic rewards had different utilities as regards job satisfaction for demographically identical subjects.

In terms of task sources, Alderfer,[111] Golembiewski,[112] Hulin and Blood,[113] Kilbridge,[114] and Bishop and Hill[115] have all shown that the key to satisfaction with aspects of the work itself (variety, amount, etc.) is dependent upon individual value systems. In each of the aforementioned studies, similar changes introduced across a number of jobs yielded different degrees of satisfaction and dissatisfaction for individual employees. Individual differences also give rise to different satisfaction levels in response to similar conditions in terms of social sources. Ingham,[116] Wofford,[117] and Goldthorpe[118] all found this to be true in their research. In the author's opinion, Turner and Lawrence[119] and Hackman and Lawler[120] have done two of the better jobs of accounting for individual differences in their research. They conclude that individual orientations toward work vary significantly across subjects. A look at the factors considered when determining 'orientations' shows them to be mainly of the social and task variety, i.e., feedback from supervisors, identity with other members, autonomy, etc. These last two studies offer strong evidence that individual differences have an impact on satisfaction from social and task sources.

The conclusion the author draws from the above studies is that different individuals will realize different satisfaction levels when exposed to identical conditions in the work environment, and that the differences can be attributed to variance in individual value systems. The key, then, appears to be the match between values and organizational rewards. Research indicates that economic rewards will be more available in larger organizations while social and task rewards will be more prevalent in smaller organizations.[121] This means that overall satisfaction levels should be the same across organization sizes since the matching of values and rewards is basically a random process, and there is no reason to suspect that members going to one size organization are any more successful than those going to another in realizing an acceptable match. In large organizations, those with value systems emphasizing economic rewards will be more satisfied than those with values favoring social and/or task rewards due to the closer value-reward match.[122] In small organizations, those whose value system emphasizes social and/or task rewards will be more satisfied than those seeking economic rewards.[123]

In total, then, the average satisfaction level for all members of any given size organization whould be the same as any other. Ingham[124] found that this condition leads to similar turnover rates across sizes. Verification of this reasoning comes from Macedonia[125] who found that when employees were given a realistic picture of the work environment prior to accepting a job, turnover rates were considerably lower. The author believes this is because they were better able to decide beforehand whether the reward system offered matched their value system.

Over time, the author suspects that the members who remain in an organization will be those with values more in congruence with the reward systems than those who leave. Thus, those in small organizations should show greater satisfaction from social and/or task sources while those in larger organizations should be more satisfied with economic rewards. As shown previously in this chapter, it is social and task values and rewards that lead to a feeling of 'attachment' to the organization and its members[126] and which is, in turn, inversely related to absenteeism among employees.[127] For this reason, organization size is hypothesized to be positively related to absenteeism.

The author hopes that it is now apparent how the literature cited in this review has led to the hypotheses put forth herein concerning size, and absenteeism and turnover rates.

Footnotes

[1] Porter, L. W., and Steers, R. M., "Organizational, Work, and Personal Factors in Employee Turnover and Absenteeism", *Psychological Bulletin*, Volume 80, 1973

[2] Ingham, G. K., *Size of Industrial Organization and Worker Behaviour*, Cambridge University Press, 1970.

[3] *Ibid.*, pg. 150.

[4] Bachman, J. G., Smith, G. C., and Slesinger, J. A., "Control, Performance, and Satisfaction: An Analysis of Structural and Individual Effects", *Journal of Personality and Social Psychology*, Volume 4, 1966.

[5] French, J. R. P., and Raven, B., "The Bases of Social Power", D. Cartwright (Ed.), *Studies in Social Power*, Ann Arbor, University of Michigan, 1959.

[6] Referent = Power based on a subordinates identification with a superior. Reward = Power derived from the ability of one individual to provide desired outcomes to another individual in exchange for compliance. Expert = Power based on the perception of one individual that another has ability, knowledge, or expertise that exceeds his own. Coercive = Power based on the ability of one individual to punish or administer negative outcomes to another. Legitimate = Power based on the position of the individual in the formal organizational hierarchy.

[7] Worthy, James, "Organizational Structure and Employee Morale", *American Sociological Review*, 1950.

[8] Weber, M., *The Theory of Social and Economic Organization*, New York: The Free Press, 1947.

[9] Question: Do you have a supervisor? . . . . Think about how you feel about your supervisor. Tell me the number of the face that shows how you feel about your supervisor.

[10] Weber, M., *The Theory of Social and Economic Organization*, New York: The Free Press, 1947.

[11] Hellriegel, D., and Slocum, J. W., Management: *A Contingency Approach*, Addison-Wesley, 1974.

[12] House, R. J., and Miner, J. B., "Merging Management and Behavioral Theory: The Interaction Between Span of Control and Group Size", *Administrative Science Quarterly*, Volume 14, 1969.

[13] Filley, A. C., and House, R. J., *Managerial Process and Organizational Behavior*, Glenview: Scott, Foresman, 1969.

[14] This is held to be true since leadership style is an important factor bearing on supervisory relations.

[15] Goldthorpe, J. H., Lockwood, D., Bechhofer, F., and Platt, J., The Affluent Worker: Industrial Attitudes and Behaviour, Cambridge, 1968; Goldthorpe, J. H., "Orientation to Work and Industrial Behaviour: A Contribution to an Acton Approach in Industrial Sociology", Unpublished paper, Cambridge, 1964.

[16] Gouldner, A. W., Patterns of Industrial Bureaucracy, London, 1955.

[17] Ibid., pg. 164.

[18] Indik, B. P., "Organization Size and Member Participation: Some Empirical Tests of Alternative Explanations", Human Relations, Volume 18, 1965.

[19] Fisher, P. H., "An Analysis of the Primary Work Group", Sociometry, Volume 16, 1953.

[20] Mayo, E., and Lombard, G. F., "Team Work and Labor Turnover in the Aircraft Industry of Southern California", Graduate School of Business, Harvard University Publications, number 32, 1944.

[21] Hellriegel, D., and Slocum, J. W., Management: A Contingency Approach, Addison-Wesley, 1974.

[22] House, R. J., and Miner, J. B., "Merging Management and Behavioral Theory: The Interaction Between Span of Control and Group Size", Administrative Science Quarterly, Volume 14, 1969.

[23] Goldthorpe, J. H., Lockwood, D., Bechhofer, F., and Platt, J., The Affluent Worker: Industrial Attitudes and Behavior, Cambridge, 1968.

[24] Mayo, E., and Lombard, G. F., "Team Work and Labor Turnover in the Aircraft Industry of Southern California", Graduate School of Business, Harvard University Publications, number 32, 1944.

[25] Hellriegel, D., and Slocum, J. W., Management: A Contingency Approach, Addison-Wesley, 1974.

[26] Beer, M., "Organizational Size and Job Satisfaction", Academy of Management Journal, Volume 7, 1964.

[27] Cleland, S., The Influence of Plant Size on Industrial Relations, Princeton, 1955.

[28] Revans, R. W., "Industrial Morale and Size of Unit", Political Quarterly, Volume 27, 1956; Revans, R. W.,"Human Relations, Management, and Size", in E. M. Hugh-Jones (Ed.), Human Relations and Modern Management, 1958.

[29] Stekler, H., Profitability and Size of Firm, Berkeley Press, 1968.

[30] Marriott, R., "Size of Work Group and Output", Occupational Psychology, Volume 26, 1949.

[31]Miner, J. B., and Miner, M. G., Personnel and Industrial Relations, Macmillan, 1973, pg. 397.

[32]Argyle, M., "Supervisory Methods Related to Productivity, Absenteeism, and Labour Turnover", Human Relations, Volume 11, 1958.

[33]Revans, R. W., "Industrial Morale and Size of Unit", Political Quarterly, Volume 27, 1956.

[34]Revans, R. W., "Human Relations, Management, and Size", in E. M. Hugh-Jones (Ed.), Human Relations and Modern Management, 1958.

[35]Herbst, P. G., "The Measurement of Behaviour Structures by Means of Input-Output Data", Human Relations, Volume 10, 1957.

[36]Porter, L. W., and Lawler, E. E., "Properties of Organization Structure in Relation to Job Attitudes and Job Behavior", Psychological Bulletin, Volume 64, 1965.

[37]Stekler, H., Profitability and Size of Firm, Berkeley Press, 1968.

[38]Locke, E. A., "Job Satisfaction and Job Performance: A Theoretical Analysis", Organizational Behavior and Human Performance, Volume 5, 1970.

[39]Bowen, D., and Siegel, P., "Relationship Between Satisfaction and Performance: The Question of Causality", Proceedings, 78th Annual Convention, American Psychological Association, 1970.

[40]Beyond a certain size, such as 5,000 members in the case of Marriott, automation will likely become a determinant of performance level. This would account for the results of both Herbst and Marriott.

[41]Marriott, R., "Size of Work Group and Output", Occupational Psychology, Volume 26, 1949.

[42]Herbst, P. G., "The Measurement of Behaviour Structures by Means of Input-Output Data", Human Relations, Volume 10, 1957.

[43]Locke, E. A., "Job Satisfaction and Job Performance: A Theoretical Analysis", Organizational Behavior and Human Performance, Volume 5, 1970.

[44]Bowen, D., and Siegel, P., "Relationship Between Satisfaction and Performance: The Question of Causality", Proceedings, 78th Annual Convention, American Psychological Association, 1970.

[45]Question: Think about how you feel about the work itself, that is, if you find your work tasks interesting or boring, or too hard or too easy, if you like or dislike them, etc. Tell me the number of the face that shows how you feel about your present tasks.

[46]Worthy, James, "Organizational Structure and Employee Morale", American Sociological Review, 1950.

[47]Filley, Allan C., "A Theory of Small Business and Divisional Growth", Unpublished Ph.D. Dissertation, Department of Business Organization, Ohio State University, 1961.

[48] Terrien, F., and Mills, D., "The Effect of Changing Size Upon the Internal Structure of Organizations", American Sociological Review, Volume 20, 1955.

[49] Thomas, E. J., and Fink, C. F., "Effects of Group Size", Psychological Bulletin, Volume 60, 1963.

[50] Worthy, James, "Organizational Structure and Employee Morale", American Sociological Review, 1950.

[51] Question: Do you work with people other than your supervisor, that is with co-workers at the same level as yourself. . .? Think about how you feel about your co-workers in general. Tell me the number of the face that shows how you feel about your co-workers.

[52] Talacchi, S., "Organizational Size, Individual Attitudes, and Behavior: An Empirical Study", Administrative Science Quarterly, Volume 5, 1960.

[53] Hewitt, D., and Parfit, J., "A Note on Working Morale and Size of Group", Occupational Psychology, Volume 27, 1953.

[54] Porter, L. W., and Lawler, E. E., "Properties of Organization Structure in Relation to Job Attitudes and Job Behavior", Psychological Bulletin, Volume 64, 1965; Kornhauser, A., Mental Health of the Industrial Worker, New York, Wiley, 1965.

[55] Rhinehart, J. B., Bassell, R. P., DeWolfe, A. S., Griffin, J. E., and Spaner, F. E., "Comparative Study of Need Satisfactions in Governmental and Business Hierarchies", Journal of Applied Psychology, Volume 53, 1969.

[56] Porter, L. W., and Mitchell, V. G., "Comparative Study of Need Satisfactions in Military and Business Hierarchies", Journal of Applied Psychology, Volume 51, 1967.

[57] Porter, L. W., "Where Is Organization Man?", Harvard Business Review, Volume 41, 1963.

[58] Subjects were questioned regarding whether they felt their work to be challenging, interesting, and whether it required any imagination.

[59] Beer, M., "Organizational Size and Job Satisfaction", Academy of Management Journal, Volume 7, 1964.

[60] Viteles, M. S., "The Two Faces of Applied Psychology", International Review of Applied Psychology, 1969.

[61] Hinrichs, J. R., "Psychology of Men at Work", Annual Review of Psychology, 1970.

[62] Locke, E. A., "What Is Job Satisfaction?", Organizational Behavior and Human Performance, Volume 4, 1969.

[63] Lawler, E. E., "Job Attitudes and Employee Motivation: Theory, Research, and Practice", Personnel Psychology, 1970.

[64] Brayfield, A. H., and Crockett, W. H., "Employee Attitudes and Employee Performance", Psychological Bulletin, 1955.

[65] Herzberg, F., Mausner, B., Peterson, R. O., and Capwell, D. F., Job Attitudes: A Review of Research and Opinion, Pittsburgh: Psychological Service of Pittsburgh, 1957.

[66] Vroom, V., Work and Motivation, New York: Wiley, 1964.

[67] Taylor, K., and Weiss, D., "Prediction of Individual Job Turnover From Measured Job Satisfaction", Proceedings of 77th Annual Convention of the American Psychological Association, 1969.

[68] For a thorough listing of all various research studies showing such a relationship the reader is referred to: Porter, L. W., and Steers, R. M., "Organizational, Work, and Personal Factors in Employee Turnover and Absenteeism", Psychological Bulletin, Volume 80, 1973.

[69] Hulin, C. L., "Job Satisfaction and Turnover in a Female Clerical Population", Journal of Applied Psychology, 1966; Hulin, C. L., "Effects of Changes in Job Satisfaction Levels on Employee Turnover", Journal of Applied Psychology, 1968.

[70] Waters, L. K., and Roach, D., "Relationship Between Job Attitudes and Two Forms of Withdrawal From the Work Situation", Journal of Applied Psychology, Volume 55, 1971.

[71] Weitz, J., and Nuckols, R. C., "Job Satisfaction and Job Survival", Journal of Applied Psychology, 1955.

[72] Mikes, P. S., and Hulin, C. L., "Use of Importance As a Weighting Component of Job Satisfaction", Journal of Applied Psychology, 1968.

[73] Wild, R., "Job Needs, Job Satisfaction and Job Behavior of Women Manual Workers", Journal of Applied Psychology, 1970.

[74] To clarify:
    If: Turnover ----- reflects ----- Satisfaction
    Then: Satisfaction - - related to - - Size
          (should be the same as)
          Turnover   - related to   - Size

[75] Ford, R. N., Motivation Through the Work Itself, New York: American Management Association, 1969.

[76] Poidevin, S. L., "A Study of Factors Affecting Labor Turnover", Personnel Practice Bulletin, Volume 1, 1949.

[77] Kerr, W. A., "Labour Turnover and Its Correlates", Journal of Applied Psychology, Volume 31, 1949.

[78] Kerr, W., Koppelmeier, G., and Sullivan, J., "Absenteeism, Turnover, and Morale in a Metals Fabrication Factory", Occupational Psychology, 1951.

[79] Metzner, H., and Mann, F., "Employee Attitudes and Absences", Personnel Psychology, Volume 6, 1953.

[80] Acton Society Trust, Size and Morale, Part II, London, 1953.

[81] Baumgartel, H., and Sobol, R., "Background and Organizational Factors in Absenteeism", Personnel Psychology, Volume 12, 1959.

[82] Indik, B. P., "Some Effects of Organization Size on Member Attitudes and Behavior", Human Relations, Volume 16, 1963.

[83] Hewitt, D., and Parfit, J., "A Note on Working Morale and Size of Group", Occupational Psychology, Volume 27, 1953.

[84] Talacchi, S., "Organizational Size, Individual Attitudes, and Behavior: An Empirical Study", Administrative Science Quarterly, Volume 5, 1960.

[85] These 'non-material' rewards included relations with management, immediate supervisors, and fellow employees.

[86] Waters, L. K., and Roach, D. "Relationship Between Job Attitudes and Two Forms of Withdrawal From the Work Situation", Journal of Applied Psychology, Volume 55, 1971.

[87] Hewitt, D., and Parfit, J., "A Note on Working Morale and Size of Group", Occupational Psychology, Volume 27, 1953.

[88] General Electric Company, Behavioral Research Service, "Attitudes Associated with Turnover of Highly Regarded Employees", Crotonville, New York, 1964 (a).

[89] Porter, L. W., and Lawler, E. E., "Properties of Organization Structure in Relation to Job Attitudes and Job Behavior", Psychological Bulletin, Volume 64, 1965.

[90] Fisher, P. H., "An Analysis of the Primary Work Group", Sociometry, Volume 16, 1953.

[91] Mayo, E., and Lombard, G. F., "Team Work and Labor Turnover in the Aircraft Industry of Southern California", Graduate School of Business, Harvard University Publications, number 32, 1944.

[92] Indik, B. P., "Some Effects of Organization Size on Member Attitudes and Behavior", Human Relations, Volume 16, 1963; Indik, B. P., "Organization Size and Member Participation: Some Empirical Tests of Alternative Explanations", Human Relations, Volume 18, 1965.

[93] Thomas, E. J., and, Fink, C. F., "Effects of Group Size", Psychological Bulletin, Volume 60, 1963.

[94] Porter, L. W., and Lawler, E. E., "Properties of Organization Structure in Relation to Job Attitudes and Job Behavior", Psychological Bulletin, Volume 64, 1965.

[95]Wofford, J. C., "The Motivational Bases of Job Satisfaction and Job Performance", Personnel Psychology, Volume 24, 1971; Ingham, G. K., Size of Industrial Organization and Worker Behaviour, Cambridge University Press, 1970.

[96]Goldthorpe, J. H., Lockwood D., Bechhofer, F., and Platt, J., The Affluent Worker: Industrial Attitudes and Behaviour, Cambridge, 1968; Hackman, J. R., and Lawler, E. E., III, "Employee Reactions to Job Characteristics", Journal of Applied Psychology, Volume 55, 1971; Wofford, J. C., "The Motivational Bases of Job Satisfaction and Job Performance", Personnel Psychology, Volume 24, 1971.

[97]Miner, J.B., The Management Process, New York, Macmillan, 1973.

[98]Ingham, G. K., Size of Industrial Organization and Worker Behaviour, Cambridge University Press, 1970.

[99]Porter, L. W., and Steers, R. M., "Organizational, Work, and Personal Factors in Employee Turnover and Absenteeism", Psychological Bulletin, Volume 80, 1973.

[100]Locke, E. A., "What Is Job Satisfaction?", Organizational Behavior and Human Performance, Volume 4, 1969.

[101]Katzell, M. E., "Expectations and Dropouts in Schools of Nursing", Journal of Applied Psychology, Volume 52, 1968.

[102]Porter, L. W., and Steers, R. M. "Organizational, Work, and Personal Factors in Employee Turnover and Absenteeism", Psychological Bulletin, Volume 80, 1973.

[103]Miner, J. B., The Management Process, New York, Macmillan, 1973.

[104]Farris, G. F., "A Predictive Study of Turnover", Personnel Psychology, Volume 24, 1971.

[105]Telly, C. S., French, W. L., and Scott, W. G., "The Relationship of Inequity to Turnover Among Hourly Workers", Administrative Science Quarterly, Volume 16, 1971.

[106]Taylor, K. E., and Weiss, D. J., "Prediction of Individual Job Turnover From Measured Job Satisfaction", Proceeding of 77th Annual Convention of the American Psychological Association, 1969.

[107]Waters, L. K., and Roach, D., "Relationship Between Job Attitudes and Two Forms of Withdrawal From the Work Situation", Journal of Applied Psychology, Volume 55, 1971.

[108]Turner, A. N., and Lawrence, P.R., "Industrial Jobs and the Worker: An Investigation of Responses to Task Attributes", Boston, Harvard University Press, Division of Research, 1965.

[109]Locke, E. A., Bryan, J. F., and Kendall, L. M., "Goals and Intentions as Mediators of the Effects of Monetary Incentive on Behavior", Journal of Applied Psychology, Volume 52, 1968.

[110]Schuster, J. R., Collette, J. A., and Knowles, L., "The Relationship Between Perceptions Concerning Magnitudes of Pay and the Perceived Utility of Pay: Public and Private Organizations Compared", Organizational Behavior and Human Performance, Volume 9, 1973.

[111]Alderfer, C. P., "An Empirical Test of a New Theory of Human Needs", Organizational Behavior and Human Performance, Volume 4, 1969; Alderfer, C. P., "Job Enlargement and the Organizational Context", Personnel Psychology, Volume 22, 1969

[112]Golembiewski, R. T., Men, Management, and Morality, New York, McGraw-Hill, 1965.

[113]Hulin, C. R., and Blood, M. R., "Job Enlargement, Individual Differences, and Worker Responses", Psychological Bulletin, Volume 60, 1968.

[114]Kilbridge, M., "Turnover, Absence, and Transfer Rates as Indicators of Employee Dissatisfaction with Reptitive Work", Industrial and Labor Relations Review, Volume 15, 1961.

[115]Bishop, R. C., and Hill, J. W., "Effects of Job Enlargement and Job Changes on Contiguous but Nonmanipulated Jobs as a Function of Workers' Status", Journal of Applied Psychology, Volume 55, 1971.

[116]Ingham, G. K., Size of Industrial Organization and Worker Behaviour, Cambridge University Press, 1970.

[117]Wofford, J. C., "The Motivational Bases of Job Satisfaction and Job Performance," Personnel Psychology, Volume 24, 1971.

[118]Goldthorpe, J. H., Lockwood, D., Bechhofer, F., and Platt, J., The Affluent Worker: Industrial Attitudes and Behaviour, Cambridge, 1968; Hackman, J. R., and Lawler, E. E., III, "Employee Reactions to Job Characteristics", Journal of Applied Psychology, Volume 55, 1971; Wofford, J. C., "The Motivational Bases of Job Satisfaction and Job Performance", Personnel Psychology, Volume 24, 1971.

[119]Turner, A. N., and Lawrence, P. R., "Industrial Jobs and the Worker: An Investigation of Responses to Task Attributes", Boston, Harvard University Press, Division of Research, 1965.

[120]Hackman, J. R., and Lawler, E. E., III, "Employee Reactions to Job Characteristics", Journal of Applied Psychology, Volume 55, 1971.

[121]Ingham, G. K., Size of Industrial Organization and Worker Behaviour, Cambridge University Press, 1970; Miner, J. B., The Management Process, New York, Macmillan, 1973; Schuster, J. R., Collette, J. A., and Knowles, L., "The Relationship Between Perceptions Concerning Magnitudes of Pay and the Perceived Utility Pay: Public and Private Organizations Compared", Organizational Behavior and Human Performance, Volume 9, 1973.

[122]Killbridge, M., "Turnover, Absence, and Transfer Rates as Indicators of Employee Dissatisfaction with Repetitive Work", Industrial and Labor Relations Review, Volume 15, 1961; Hewitt, D., and Parfit, J., "A Note on Working Morale and Size of Group", Occupational Psychology, Volume 27, 1953.

[123]Sexton, W. P., "Organizational and Individual Needs: A Conflict?", Personnel Journal, Volume 46, 1967; Hewitt, D., and Parfit, J., "A Note on Working Morale and Size of Group", Occupational Psychology, Volume 27, 1953.

[124]Ingham, G. K., Size of Industrial Organization and Worker Behaviour, Cambridge University Press, 1970; Ingham, G. K., "Organization Size, Orientation to Work and Industrial Behaviour", Sociology, Volume 1, 1967.

[125]Macedonia, R. M., "Expectation--Press and Survival", Unpublished Doctoral Dissertation, Graduate School of Public Administration, New York University, June 1969.

[126]Talacchi, S., "Organization Size, Individual Attitudes, and Behavior: An Empirical Study", Administrative Science Quarterly, Volume 5, 1960; Hewitt, D., and Parfit, J., "A Note on Working Morale and Size of Group", Occupational Psychology, Volume 27, 1953; Ingham, G. K., Size of Industrial Organization and Worker Behaviour, Cambridge University Press, 1970.

[127]Kerr, W., Koppelmeier, G., and Sullivan, J., "Absenteeism, Turnover, and Morale in a Metals Fabrication Factory", Occupational Psychology, 1951; Metzner, H., and Mann, F., "Employee Attitudes and Absences", Personnel Psychology, Volume 6, 1953; Acton Society Trust, Size and Morale, Part II, London, 1953; Baumgartel, H., and Sobol, R., "Background and Organizational Factors in Absenteeism", Personnel Psychology, Volume 12, 1959.

III METHODOLOGY

A cross section of employees and organizations involved in solid waste management are used as subjects in this book. For purposes of data collection organizations were randomly sampled and were stratified along lines of geographic region, city size (based on the Standard Metropolitan Statistical Area system with cities randomly selected within each stratum), and whether they were publically or privately owned (with random sampling within each stratum for each city selected).

This sampling yielded 3,327 organizations, which were then asked to allow one management representative to be interviewed concerning management policies. Additionally, in approximately 30% of the organizations, permission was asked to conduct one employee interview. Stratifying variables in the employee sample are geographic region, public versus private ownership, and job levels of managerial (N=61), clerical (N=75), supervisory/foreman (N=146), skilled labor (N=303), unskilled labor (N=326). Within each organization, the employee was chosen at random from the job category desired, and the sample size is in proportion to the estimated number of employees at each level in the total population.

In this investigation, employees used as subjects are either skilled (N=295) or unskilled (N=315) blue collar workers.

Thus, responses to a structured interview were the source of data.[1] Questions fall within one of the following four areas:

>demographic
>
>present job information
>
>rewards offered by the organization
>
>individual attitudes

Basic information needed concerned organization size, absenteeism, turnover, overall level of job satisfaction, and individual components or sources of such satisfaction.

A question regarding the size of the organization was included at the beginning of the interview form:

Size of Organization _____

For purposes of statistical analysis organizations were classified as either 'large' or 'small' based on a breakpoint of 75 employees. The choosing of any such point is admittedly somewhat arbitrary, yet Caplow[2] states that the relationship between size and level of bureaucracy is other than linear, and that until the number of employees begins to approach 100, the formal and social structures of the organization do not necessarily have to become bureaucratized. In Ingham's[3] classification of his eight plants, the small organizations have up to 63 members and the large as few as 90 in the particular departments he studied.[4]

Number of Employees

Small Organizations	Large Organizations
1 - 75	76 and above (actual sample includes organizations of over 2,000 employees)

The question of public or private ownership was controlled for by using information from the following question.

Type of Organization (CHECK ONE)

Private ( )

Public {
City ( )
County ( )
State ( )
Federal ( )
}

Private and publically owned organizations within each size classification were studied separately.

Absenteeism data was, likewise, obtained directly and early in the questionnaire from the following question:

Working days absent in the last six months (COUNT SICK LEAVE AND LEAVE WITHOUT PAY BUT NOT ANNUAL LEAVE) _____

Employee responses to this question were checked against those given by management for the particular employee. Later in the questionnaire the worker was asked:

How many days do you typically work per week? _____

This information was then used in the following manner.

$$\text{Total absence} = \frac{\text{Total Days Lost, Last Six Months}}{\text{Total Days Scheduled To Be Worked}} \times 100$$

"Total days scheduled to be worked" was obtained by multiplying the number of days typically worked per week by a factor of twenty-six (the weeks in a six-month period).

As regards turnover, this study deals with intended, or projected, figures. Each subject was asked the following question:

Do you hope to be working in the solid waste management field (e.g., refuse, scrap) five (5) years from now?

> Yes ( )
>
> No ( )

The percent of 'yes' and 'no' responses for subjects in organizations within each category was then compared. It should be noted, however, that the question dealt with the entire solid waste management field. It would be possible for the respondent to change jobs while remaining in the same occupation. For that reason, the following question was, likewise, asked:

How much longer do you intend to work for this organization?

_____yr. _____mo.

For purposes of analysis, a breakpoint of five years was used, so as to coincide with intended turnover in the previous question. The percent of subjects intending to stay less or longer than five years was compared across the two size categories.

A third question was also asked, immediately after the above question on intended longevity.

Is this up to the age of retirement?

        Yes   ( )

        No   ( )

Those respondents who indicated they would work for less than five years, but up to the age of retirement were not considered in calculations regarding intended longevity. The percentage of workers in each size organization (large and small) who intended to stay with their present employer until age of retirement was compared.

As Ingham[5] points out, the turnover rate alone may not be an adequate measure, as a few undesirable jobs may account for a disproportionately high percentage of the final figure. This was not a consideration for this study, however, since figures here were for projected quits, meaning that at the time the questionnaire was completed an undesirable job could account for only one quit, the incumbent. In Ingham's case, where past quits are used, an undesirable job could, as he points out, account for a number of quits.

Dispite this, Ingham's second measure of turnover was used in this study. The author felt it conveyed information concerning the 'organizational attachment' mentioned earlier, and it was included for that reason.

Subjects were asked the following question:

How long have you worked here? _____yrs. _____mos.
This information was then used to derive a "stability rate", defined as follows:

$$\text{Stability Rate} = \frac{\text{Number of Workers with Over 5 Years Service}}{\text{Number of Respondents within the Particular Size Classification}}$$

Thus, turnover data came from the three questions regarding the five year projection, intended longevity, and plans until retirement age. Stability rates came from the above question regarding time already worked with the present employer.

At this point, organization size was correlated with total absence measures as well as turnover and stability rates.

To explain the relationships, or lack thereof, found between size and absenteeism and turnover rates, levels and sources of job satisfaction were used. The intent here was to use both quantity and quality of satisfaction to explain the previously found correlations.

One measure of the overall level of job satisfaction was a summation of the employee's attitudes toward specific sources of satisfaction. The employee was given a card with seven faces on it. The expressions on the faces went from a deep frown indicating extreme dissatisfaction to a deep smile indicating extreme satisfaction. Under each face, there was a number from one to seven, with the more 'satisfied' faces having the higher numbers.[6] The employee was then asked to tell the interviewer the number under the face which showed how satisfied or dissatisfied he was with each of the things he was being asked about. He was asked the following questions (with appropriate explanatory remarks):

Think about how you feel about your <u>supervisor</u>. Tell me the number of the face that shows how you feel about your supervisor.

_____

Think about how you feel about your <u>co-workers</u> in general. Tell me the number of the face that shows how you feel about your co-workers.

_____

Tell me the number of the face that shows how satisfied or dissatisfied you are with the <u>subordinates</u> you work with.

_____

(asked
You said that your present take home <u>pay</u> comes to about . . . .
    earlier)
. . . . a week. Tell me the number of the face that shows how you feel about your pay.

_____

You said that the organization (or union) provides the following
    (asked earlier)
benefits . . . . Think about how satisfied or dissatisfied you are with these benefits. Tell me the number of the face that shows how you feel about the benefits you get here.

_____

Now lets talk about <u>promotions</u>. You said that so far you have
    (asked earlier)
received . . . . promotions, and think your chances
                    (asked earlier)
of getting another within two years are . . . . . . Would you like more chances for promotion than you have now or are you satisfied

with the way things are . . . .? Tell me the number of the face that shows how you feel about your promotion opportunities here.

_____

Think about how you feel about the work itself, that is, if you find your work tasks interesting or boring, or too hard or too easy, if you like them or dislike them, etc. Tell me the number of the face that shows how you feel about your present tasks.

_____

Do you have any variety on this job, that is, do you have a chance to do many different kinds of things, or do you do the same thing every day . . . .? Would you like more variety or are you satisfied with the amount you have now . . . .? Tell me the number of the face that shows how you feel about the amount of variety on your job.

_____

How is the amount of work on your job on a typical day? Do you have just the right amount or do you have too much or too little to do . . . .? Tell me the number of the face that shows how satisfied or dissatisfied you are with the amount of work you have on this job on a typical day.

_____

Tell me the number of the face that shows how satisfied or dissatisfied you are with each of the following:
a) the equipment you use on your job. _____
b) the hours of work. _____
As previously stated, the sum of the numbers given for each of

these questions was used as a measure of overall job satisfaction. This measure was then related to organization size to show similarities or differences in employee satisfaction across various sized organizations. This information was, in turn, used to explain the size-turnover relationship.

Absenteeism was viewed here not as a manifestation of overall satisfaction level but of the 'attachment' or 'commitment' to work spoken of earlier. This feeling of attachment was felt to be enhanced by the presence of social and task rewards such as favorable interpersonal relations with supervisors, co-workers, subordinates, the work itself, amount of work, and variety on the job.

The sources or components of satsifaction mentioned above were classified as either 'economic', 'social', or 'task'. The three questions concerning pay, benefits, and promotions were classified as economically oriented while the three concerning relations with supervisors, co-workers, and subordinates were considered social. The questions regarding the work itself, variety on job, and the amount of work were considered 'task' oriented. Satisfaction from each individual source and within each of these three groups was then related to organization size. This information was, in turn, used to explain the size-absenteeism relationship.

The categorization of each type answer within one of the three general areas, i.e., those relating to pay, benefits, or promotions as 'economic', etc., was done based on the author's review of the literature in this area.[7] To coincide as closely as possible to Ingham's[8] particular classification, the responses were recounted eliminating promotions, subordinates, and amount of work from the economic, social, and task tabulations respectively.

In addition to the above mentioned eleven sources of satisfaction, responses to additional questions were also correlated with the size factor. A single, indirect measure of overall satisfaction was derived from responses to the following question:

If you had your life to live over, would you like to wind up in the same line of work as the one you're in now?

        Yes   ( )

        No   ( )

The number of positive and negative responses in large and small organizations were compared. This information was, in turn, used (along with the sum of the numbers for each of the 'faces' questions) to explain the size-turnover relationship.

Employees were also asked the following question:

Now would you try to think of a specific time when you were especially _satisfied_ with your present job, a time when you felt especially _good_ about your job. Can you think of such a time? (IF NOT PROBE) . . . . Exactly what happened to make you feel good? Who or what was mainly responsible for this event?

Responses were classified according to the categories on page 136 of the Coders Manual (Appendix B), Good Day Event Categories. Responses that fell within categories 05 and 08 (Promotion and Money) were considered economic. Responses within categories 07 and 09 (Verbal Recognition and Interpersonal Atmosphere) were considered social. Responses within categories 01, 02, 03, and 04 (Task Activity, Amount of Work, Smoothness of Work, Success) were taken to relate to task.

A second tabulation was then run eliminating Promotions and Amount of Work from the economic and task categories so as to duplicate Ingham's categorization.

Later in the interview employees were asked:

What two things about this job give you the most pleasure? What two things make you happiest about your job here?

1. _____

2. _____

Responses were classified according to the categories on page 141 of the Coders Manual (Appendix B). Responses that fell within categories 04 and 05 (Promotions and Pay) were considered economic. Those which fell within categories 06, 07 and 08 (Supervisor, Co-workers, Subordinates) were considered social. Those within categories 00, 01, 02, and 03 (Work Itself, Success, Smoothness of Work, Amount of Work) were taken to relate to task.

Again a second tabulation was run, eliminating Promotions, Amount of Work, and Subordinates from the count, for the reasons already detailed.

Additionally, subjects were asked:

How did you come to work in the solid waste management field? What made you decide to work in this field? _____

_____

_____

Responses were classified according to the categories on page 134 of the Coders Manual (Appendix B). Responses that fell within categories 0 and 5 (Pay/benefits/job security, Chance(s) for advancement) were considered economic. Those which fell within categories 2 and 6 (Relative(s) or friend(s) in field, Supervision) were considered social. Those which fell within category 3 (Type of work) were considered task related. The second tabulation, in accordance with Ingham, eliminated 'Chances for Advancement'.

Three index numbers were computed from the four responses of each subject, indicating the number of these responses classified as economic, social, and task (0, 1, 2, 3, 4). Composite number for all those employees in organizations classified as large and small were then computed and compared for all three sources. This process was repeated twice, once with promotions, subordinates, and amount of work considered, and once without. Additionally, comparisons were made across sizes for each individual response, without the grouping process described above.

Information from these three questions was studied to give an insight into the respondents orientation toward work. The more often economic, social, or task sources were indicated as responses to these questions, the more important that particular aspect of the job was felt to be for the individual subject. This information concerning orientation toward work was then related to the amount of satisfaction from corresponding sources with the intent of explaining the size-absenteeism relationship. (For a further explanation of how this information was used, see Hypothesis section of Introduction).

Finally, information concerning the actual rate of pay and number of benefits for each subject was gathered and used in conjunction with economic satisfaction and orientation measures from the open ended questions. It was hypothesized that the closeness of the match between actual level of compensation and number of benefits and the value placed on such economic rewards would be reflected in satisfaction levels from economic sources. For this reason subjects were asked the following questions:

What is your present hourly pay $_____hr.

If subjects failed to answer this question, the information was obtained from responses to the following two questions:

What is your present gross pay per week, that is, before deductions?
$_____wk.

How many hours is your typical week? _____hrs.

Responses to the latter question were divided into the former to arrive at an hourly rate.

Additionally, subjects were questioned concerning the number of benefits received as follows:

Do you get (have) (PLACE CHECK IN APPROPRIATE BOX)

		yes	no
a)	Medical/surgical benefits here?	( )	( )
b)	Sick leave with pay?	( )	( )
c)	Paid holidays (Xmas, etc.)?	( )	( )
d)	Paid vacations or annual leave?	( )	( )
e)	A retirement or pension plan?	( )	( )
f)	Group life insurance?	( )	( )
g)	Profit sharing?	( )	( )
h)	Workmen's Compensation?	( )	( )
i)	A credit union?	( )	( )
j)	Any other benefits? (SPECIFY) _____	( )	( )
k)	_____	( )	( )

(TOTAL # OF "YES'S" = _____)

In summary, then, investigated herein is the relationship between organizations of various sizes and rates of absenteeism and turnover. The hypothesis is that differences in these two rates will be manifestations of different satisfaction levels and sources of satisfaction between organizations.

Footnotes

[1] A copy of the Questionnaire and Coders Manual are included as Appendices A and B, respectively.

[2] Caplow, T., "Organization Size", Administrative Science Quarterly, Volume 1, 1957.

[3] Ingham, G. K., Size of Industrial Organization and Worker Behaviour, Cambridge University Press, 1970, pg. 19.

[4] In the large organizations, overall company size was 3,000-5,000.

[5] Ingham, G. K., Size of Industrial Organization and Worker Behaviour, Cambridge University Press, 1970, pg. 23.

[6] The card can be seen in Appendix B, page 144.

[7] Worthy, James, "Organizational Structure and Employee Morale", American Sociological Review, 1950; Filley, A. C., and House, R. J., Managerial Process and Organizational Behavior, Glenview: Scott, Foresman, 1969; Goldthorpe, J. H., "Orientation to Work and Industrial Behaviour: A Contribution to an Acton Approach in Industrial Sociology", Unpublished Paper, Cambridge, 1964.

[8] Ingham, G. K., Size of Industrial Organization and Worker Behaviour, Cambridge University Press, 1970.

IV STATISTICAL ANALYSIS AND FINDINGS

Before presenting the results of the statistical analysis, the basic premises of the author will be briefly recapitulated.

The basic thesis is that as organization size increases, workers attachment to the organization, as measured by absenteeism, decreases overall job satisfaction and its corollary, turnover, are expected to be unaffected.

Feelings of attachment or identification with the organization as manifested by absenteeism are hypothesized to be positively related to the match between quantity of job satisfaction derived from social and task sources, and the importance of these sources as determined by the particular individuals "orientation toward work".[1]

Based on prior research, smaller organizations are felt to be better able to foster feelings of attachment through social and task sources, and, hence, are expected to show lower absenteeism rates. Larger organizations are not seen as able to offer social and task rewards but rather are expected to emphasize economic rewards more, thus reversing the above process and leading to higher absenteeism rates.[2]

Despite the fact that job satisfaction sources vary with organization size, the overall level of job satisfaction is expected to remain constant across sizes.[3] Since overall job satisfaction levels are felt to be reflected in turnover rates, such rates are hypothesized to remain constant across various sizes.

A sample of at least one management representative from 3,327 different organizations and one non-managerial employee from over 1,000 organizations was administered either the management or employee questionnaire. The results are used to test the hypotheses put forth above. For purposes of the present study, the portion of the sample used is 610 employees, stratified by organization size,[4] public or private ownership, and skilled or unskilled job· classifications.

All statistical tests are, therefore, run on each of the following ten categories:

Table 4.1: Categorization of Subjects

Category Number	Stratification Characteristics	Group Size
1	Size (Small)	N = 463
2	Size (Small) and Ownership (Private)	N = 316
3	Size (Small) and Ownership (Public)	N = 147
4	Size (Small) and Skill Level (Unskilled)	N = 233
5	Size (Small) and Skill Level (Skilled)	N = 230
6	Size (Large)	N = 147
7	Size (Large) and Ownership (Private)	N = 62
8	Size (Large) and Ownership (Public)	N = 85
9	Size (Large) and Skill Level (Unskilled)	N = 82
10	Size (Large) and Skill Level (Skilled)	N = 65

The primary distinction for purposes of this study concerns differences between categories one and six. When analyzing the results for significant differences, not only categories one and six, but also two and seven, three and eight, four and nine, and five and ten are compared in order to determine the possible moderating effect of these other factors.

The first piece of statistical information the author extracted from the data concerned absenteeism rates. The total days absent for the last six months was divided by the total days scheduled to be worked by all employees in each category as indicated by responses to both the employment and management questionnaire, and the result multiplied by 100 to arrive at an index of absenteeism. Having done this, steps were taken to insure that a few select individuals could not be distorting the index for various categories by virtue of a single prolonged absence, since the index accounts for number of days but not number of separate incidents of absence. It was obvious from even a cursory analysis of the figures that a few subjects were extremely unrepresentative as regards their rates of absenteeism. For example, the top 1.5% of categories one and six accounted for 24.3% of the absenteeism. It seems a justifiable assumption that anyone absent for 25 working days in six months had at least one prolonged unavoidable absence. This study is not concerned with these prolonged, unavoidable absences due to sickness, accidents, etc. Additionally, with one exception, no subject with less than 25 days absence had more than 17. Thus, when the data was plotted 25 was the obvious breakpoint. For these reasons, the index was run again for categories one and six eliminating those subjects with more than 25 days absence in the last six months. The results are presented in Table 4.2.

Table 4.2: Absenteeism Index

Category	Total Index	Adjusted Index	Avg. Work Week (Days)
1	2.069**[5]	1.386 (N.S.)	5.28
2	2.025*	---	5.34
3	2.165**	---	5.16
4	2.286**	---	5.27
5	1.850 (N.S.)	---	5.29
6	2.578	1.604	5.12
7	1.554	---	5.24
8	3.313	---	5.04
9	3.275	---	5.06
10	1.633	---	5.12

*p < .05
**p < .01

The reader is reminded that significance levels are for differences between categories one-six, two-seven, three-eight, four-nine, and five-ten.

As can be seen from Table 4.2, the hypothesized difference between large and small organizations concerning absenteeism rates emerged as predicted when the entire sample was considered. The variables of type of ownership and skill level caused inconsistent results when combined with the major variable of size, with small organizations having lower rates when publically owned and large concerns showing lower rates when held privately. Unskilled employees are absent more in large organizations, while there is no significant difference based on size for skilled workers. When the adjusted sample (those with less than 25 days absence) was used the relationship was again in the hypothesized direction, although not statistically significant. The important point to be made here is that the absenteeism relationship was in the hypothesized direction at a significant level for the combined subjects in large and small organizations.

As regards turnover, the author dealt first with intended or projected figures. Three separate measures of turnover were gathered for each subject, the first concerning whether they hoped to be working in the solid waste management field five years from now, the second concerning intended longevity with the present employer, and the third dealing with employment plans until retirement age. The results for the first of these questions are presented below:

Table 4.3: Do you hope to be working in the solid waste management field five (5) years from now?

Category	% Yes	% No
1	77.0*	23.0*
2	73.5*	26.5*
3	84.4 (N.S.)	15.6 (N.S.)
4	74.1*	25.9 (N.S.)
5	79.8 (N.S.)	20.2 (N.S.)
6	86.3	13.7
7	88.5	11.5
8	84.7	15.3
9	89.0	11.0
10	82.8	17.2

*$p < .01$

For this particular measure of projected turnover, then, employees in smaller organizations expressed a greater willingness to leave the field than those in larger organizations. In all five comparisons, the relationship is in the same direction, although not always significant. It is seen to be significant in the major comparison of groups one and six. Regardless of ownership or skill level, those in smaller firms were more willing to leave the field than those in larger. Thus, size seems to be the main variable relating to willingness to stay in the field. The ownership and skill variables show inconsistent results in that in small organizations, privately owned concerns and unskilled employees were less willing to stay in the same line of work, while just the opposite was true in large concerns. The important point to be made here, however, is that this measure dealt with intent to remain in the solid waste field rather than to remain with the particular employing organization, the latter being that unit which was of immediate concern for this study. It would be entirely possible for a respondent to change employers while remaining in the same occupation or field. For this reason, the subjects were also questioned concerning how long they intended to work for their present employer. So as to coincide with intended turnover in the previous question, a breakpoint of five years was used. Employees were also asked if this was up to retirement age. If it was, but was, likewise, less than five years, they were not included in the following tabulation. The results are presented in Table 4.4.

Table 4.4: How much longer do you intend to work for this organization? Is this up to the age of retirement?[6]

Category	% Over 5 Years	% 5 Years or Under	% Until Retire
1	73.3**	23.8**	69.0**
2	66.0*	31.9*	62.1*
3	86.9 (N.S.)	8.5 (N.S.)	83.6 (N.S.)
4	69.2*	28.1*	67.8**
5	77.0 (N.S.)	20.0 (N.S.)	70.2*
6	83.3	12.5	82.6
7	82.6	17.4	78.3
8	83.8	9.5	85.7
9	85.1	12.3	85.5
10	81.4	12.7	78.6

*$p < .01$
**$p < .001$

All significant results show, as in the case of the previous question concerning the entire field, that employees in smaller organizations expressed a stronger probability of leaving the organization than those in larger organizations. This relationship held for private ownership and unskilled employees. No significant results in any category were counter to the main one-six comparison. Similarly, in all significant cases, employees in larger organizations were more likely to remain until retirement than those in smaller ones. Both these relationships are particularly strong in the important category one-category six comparison.

An additional measure of turnover was also used, referred to as the "stability rate",[7] a measure centering around past rather than projected, longevity with the present employer. For purposes of consistency, five years was again used as the breakpoint, with the results presented below:

Table 4.5: Stability Rate

Category	Rate
1	28.6**
2	22.5*
3	40.1*
4	23.3*
5	33.5*
6	43.8
7	35.5
8	48.2
9	36.9
10	50.8

*$p < .01$
**$p < .001$

Again, in all cases, greater stability is exhibited by those in larger organizations. These various results concerning stability and intended turnover disagree with the previously stated hypothesis regarding the lack of any relationship between these factors and organization size. The author's explanation of the findings regarding these two factors is one of the main concerns of the final chapter.

At this point, correlations were run between organization size and measures of absenteeism, turnover, and longevity.

To remain internally consistent and to minimize the effects of the situation described preceeding Table 4.2, the correlations were first run as point biserials with size dichotomized as large or small. For absenteeism, the results was a correlation of +.187 ($p < .001$), for longevity +.231 ($p < .001$), and for intended turnover +.066 ($p < .05$). Next, the tests were rerun with size broken into ten categories (see page 124 of the Coders Manual, Appendix B) as a crosscheck of the biserial results. For all three measures, the results

were not significantly different from those of the point biserial tests.
When absenteeism was run on the ten category size classification with the
25 day cut-off the result was a coefficient of +.289 (P < .001). These results
are consistent with those presented in Tables 4.2 through 4.5 despite some
obvious differences in categorization of the data. For instance, Table 4.2
contains 'standardized' data on absenteeism because of the denominator used,
while for correlation purposes 'total days absent, last six months' was
used without standardization.

As regards measures of longevity and stability, in all three previous
cases (Tables 4.3-4.5) a five year breakpoint was used with subjects classified
as either over or under this figure. As opposed to this dichotomous classification used previously, the stability and longevity variables were discrete
for purposes of the correlation analysis, with responses rounded to the
nearest year. The results for longevity are consistent with those presented in Table 4.5, with stability increasing as size increases. As regards
intended turnover, the results of the correlation analysis are again
consistent with those arrived at with a dichotomous classification of
responses. In this case, however, the author feels it necessary to
provide a brief interpretation of the results. The subjects were asked
how much longer they intended to work for their present employer. The
figure used for purposes of analysis was their response rounded to the
nearest year.[8] Those in larger organizations indicated they would be
staying a greater number of years than those in smaller ones, and this
is reflected in the positive nature of the correlation coefficient. The
label of "turnover" as applied to responses regarding the particular
question may mislead some readers, since what was analyzed was a projected
yearly figure, not the number of individuals actually leaving.

Thus, based on past and projected performance, subjects in larger organizations tend to work longer periods of time with an individual employer than those in smaller organizations. As stated in Chapter I, the author did not expect to find differences in stability and turnover rates across the size variable, and while the correlation coefficient is very small, the 11.3% difference (Table 4.4) when responses are dichotomized is significant.

At this point, the author reiterates that various forms of satisfaction were felt to provide an explanation of absenteeism and turnover rates. Total satisfaction was felt to be reflected in turnover rates while satisfaction from social and task sources were felt to impact on absenteeism rates. Correlations were run between measures of total days absent for the last six months and the subjects responses to the "faces" questions concerning amount and source of job satisfaction.[9] Tests were run once with and once without promotions, amount of work, and subordinates considered as sources of economic, task, and social satisfaction, respectively, as per the discussion in the Methodology Chapter. They were also run once with all subjects and once excluding the top .015 of subjects in terms of days absent.[10] The results are presented below:

Table 4.6: Correlation Between Total Absence and Degree of Satisfaction From Various Sources: All Subjects

Absence Correlated With	Satisfaction With										
	Work Itself	Supervision	Co-Workers	Subordinates	Benefits	Pay	Promotions	Variety	Amount of Work	Equipment	Hours of Work	Total
Economic Sources	N.S.	N.S.	N.S.	N.S.	-.0801**	-.0913**	-.1131**					-.1204**
Social Sources	-.0851*	N.S.	N.S.	N.S.				N.S.			N.S.	-.0997**
Task Sources								N.S.	-.1356**			-.0788*
Social and Task Sources	-.1503**	N.S.	N.S.	N.S.				N.S.	-.1390**			-.1012**
Economic Sources		-.0658*	-.0565*		-.0807*	-.0915**						-.0790*
Social Sources	-.0851*							N.S.				-.0600*
Task Sources								N.S.				-.0799*
Social and Task Sources	-.0899*	-.0691*	-.0567*					N.S.				-.0799*
Total Satisfaction	-.1493**	N.S.	N.S.	N.S.	-.1211*	-.1427**	-.0639*	N.S.	-.1359**	N.S.	N.S.	-.1226*

*p < .05
**p < .001

{Included}
{Excluded}

Table 4.7: Correlation Between Total Absence and Degree of Satisfaction From Various Sources: 25 Day Cut-off

Satisfaction With

Absence Correlated With	Work Itself	Supervision	Co-Workers	Subordinates	Benefits	Pay	Promotions	Variety	Amount of Work	Equipment	Hours of Work	Total
Excluded												
Economic Sources		-.0961*	-.0671*	N.S.	-.0689*	-.0909**	-.1244**					-.1211**
Social Sources	-.1188**		-.0987*	N.S.								-.0972*
Task Sources	-.0504*			N.S.				-.1226**	-.0875*			-.1465**
Social and Task Sources						-.0697*						-.1083*
Included												
Economic Sources		-.1162**	-.0635*			-.0910**						-.0948**
Social Sources	-.1188**							-.1226**				-.1177**
Task Sources								N.S.	-.0875*			-.1134**
Social and Task Sources	-.1239**	-.1226**	-.0642*					-.1184**	-.1239**			-.1563*
Total Satisfaction	N.S.	-.0977*	-.0735*	N.S.		-.0662*	-.0672*	N.S.	-.0775*	N.S.	N.S.	-.0939**

*p < .05
**p < .001

As can be seen from the above two tables, overall job satisfaction was negatively correlated with absenteeism (-.1226, p < .05), as hypothesized. Likewise, satisfaction with social and task sources combined correlated with absenteeism as predicted (-.0788, -.0799, -.1088, -.1561, all p < .05) for the four respective tests, i.e., including and excluding questions concerning amount of work, promotions, and subordinates, both for all subjects and with the twenty-five day cut-off on absenteeism.

Since absenteeism was found to be less in smaller organizations (Table 4.2), and, hence, positively correlated with size (+.182, p < .001), and since both total satisfaction and satisfaction from social and task sources combined are negatively correlated with absenteeism, one should expect to find these satisfaction measures to be higher in smaller organizations. Responses to the 'faces' questions were analyzed by the original ten category breakout to find if this was, indeed, the case. Here again the tests were run with and without the three questions concerning promotions, amount of work, and subordinates. Totals given in the table are with [(3) and (6)] and without [(2) and (4)] these questions. Figures in the body represent the average response for all subjects in the category for the particular question, with a range of 1 (Extremely Dissatisfied) to 7 (Extremely Satisfied).

Table 4.8: Satisfaction From Various Sources, Across Organization Size

Category	Economic				Social				Task				Total, Social, Task (4)	Total, Social, Task (6)	Total (11)
	Benefits	Pay	Total (2)	Promotions	Total (3)	Supervisor	Co-Workers	Total (2)	Subordinates	Total (3)	Variety	Work Itself	Total (2)	Amount of Work	Total (3)	
1	5.27 (N.S.)	4.82**	5.06**	4.72*	4.96**	6.07 (N.S.)	6.13 (N.S.)	6.10 (N.S.)	6.02 (N.S.)	6.09 (N.S.)	5.54*	5.70*	5.62*	5.45*	5.56**	5.86*	5.80**	5.65**
2	5.02 (N.S.)	4.89 (N.S.)	4.95 (N.S.)	4.83 (N.S.)	4.91 (N.S.)	6.10 (N.S.)	6.08 (N.S.)	6.09 (N.S.)	6.08 (N.S.)	6.08 (N.S.)	5.62 (N.S.)	5.72 (N.S.)	5.67 (N.S.)	5.40*	5.59**	5.88 (N.S.)	5.80*	5.43 (N.S.)
3	5.82**	4.66**	5.23**	4.50	4.90**	6.01 (N.S.)	6.27 (N.S.)	6.13 (N.S.)	6.06 (N.S.)	6.12 (N.S.)	5.38 (N.S.)	5.66 (N.S.)	5.52**	5.59*	5.28**	5.78 (N.S.)	5.75**	5.59**
4	5.21 (N.S.)	4.79**	5.29*	4.78*	4.92**	6.07 (N.S.)	6.16 (N.S.)	6.11 (N.S.)	6.19 (N.S.)	6.12 (N.S.)	5.39 (N.S.)	5.52 (N.S.)	5.46 (N.S.)	5.33*	5.42*	5.78 (N.S.)	5.72*	5.39*
5	5.34 (N.S.)	4.86**	5.09**	4.66 (N.S.)	4.95*	6.08 (N.S.)	6.16 (N.S.)	6.11 (N.S.)	5.94 (N.S.)	6.05 (N.S.)	5.70 (N.S.)	5.88 (N.S.)	5.79 (N.S.)	5.55 (N.S.)	5.71*	5.90*	5.87*	5.32 (N.S.)
6	5.10	4.05	4.57	4.33	4.49	6.10	6.12	6.18	5.76	6.01	5.29	5.48	5.38	5.06	5.27	5.73	5.62	5.32
7	4.95	4.52	4.73	4.63	4.70	6.23	6.13	6.18	5.74	6.05	5.52	5.63	5.57	4.92	5.35	5.87	5.69	5.34
8	5.21	3.72	4.45	4.12	4.34	6.07	6.01	6.04	5.74	5.94	5.38	5.36	5.24	5.13	5.20	5.69	5.57	5.20
9	5.11	4.07	4.59	4.25	4.48	6.17	6.27	6.22	5.72	6.04	5.12	5.32	5.22	4.85	5.10	5.72	5.55	5.17
10	5.08	4.03	4.54	4.44	4.51	6.02	5.97	5.99	5.78	5.93	5.51	5.68	5.60	5.30	5.50	5.79	5.70	5.38

* p < .05
** p < .001

Totals are not exact averages of figures on individual questions due to changes in the number of responses per question.

As can be seen from the above table, satisfaction from social and task sources combined is higher in smaller organizations, with the difference being accounted for by the task area. No significant difference is evidenced for any group across the social sources. This partially explains the difference in absenteeism across size and is consistent with the correlations between size and absenteeism. The same points can be made concerning total satisfaction, which is, likewise, higher in smaller organizations. Despite the fact that this difference in overall job satisfaction levels explains earlier findings, it was not originally expected by the author.[12]

Except for the fact that skilled employees expressed greater satisfaction with task sources, no significant nor consistent difference appears between the two variables of ownership and skill level.

As a check on overall satisfaction levels, subjects were asked one general question regarding their willingness to relive their lives in the same occupation. It was hoped that this would provide a rough measure of overall job satisfaction. The results are presented below:

Table 4.9: If you had your life to live over, would you like to wind up in the same line of work as the one you're doing now?

Category	Would	Would Not
1	52.52%*	47.48%*
2	53.21% (N.S.)	46.79% (N.S.)
3	51.03% (N.S.)	48.97% (N.S.)
4	47.83% (N.S.)	52.17% (N.S.)
5	57.27% (N.S.)	42.73% (N.S.)
6	46.90%	53.10%
7	49.18%	50.82%
8	45.24%	54.76%
9	42.86%	57.14%
10	52.46%	47.54%

* $p < .1$
N.S. - all between .15-.29

While the final four comparisons are not statistically significant, they are all in the same direction, and the most important comparison is significant. This finding is consistent with those presented in Tables 4.8 and 4.2.

The statistics thus far show internal consistency, yet at the same time fail to support one of the original hypotheses of the author. It was felt that turnover levels would not be significantly different across the size variable, yet as Tables 4.4 and 4.5 clearly show, there are statistically significant differences, with smaller organizations having higher turnover and lower stability rates.

This finding leads to the obvious question of whether overall job satisfaction and turnover/stability rates are, indeed, correlated. The answer is that they are, but to a lesser degree than originally expected. Figures in the body of the Table below are correlation coefficients.

Table 4.10: Correlation: Overall Satisfaction-Turnover, Stability

	Overall Satisfaction
Turnover (All orgs.)	.1285**[13]
Turnover (Small orgs.)	.2081**
Turnover (Large orgs.)	-.0054 (N.S.)
Stability (All orgs.)	.0972**
Stability (Small orgs.)	.1144**
Stability (Large orgs.)	.1278*

* $p < .05$
**$p < .001$

As can be seen from Table 4.10, turnover was more highly correlated with job satisfaction levels in small, rather than large organizations, while the coefficients are similar for stability in both categories. The magnitude of the coefficients across all groups is explained by earlier findings showing that while stability increases with size (Table 4.5), total satisfaction decreases (Table 4.8). Likewise, despite this lesser level of job satisfaction, those in larger organizations indicated they intended to stay a greater number of years than did their counterparts in smaller organizations (Table 4.4).

Thus, overall job satisfaction is seen to be related to stability and turnover rates, as originally hypothesized, yet there was not the similarity expected across size concerning levels of job satisfaction. Concerning satisfaction from specific sources, the higher levels from task sources expected in smaller organizations was, indeed, found, yet the difference in satisfaction from economic sources was in the opposite direction of what was originally thought to be the case (Table 4.8). It is this latter situation that accounts for the unexpected results in overall satisfaction levels.

Here again, these results are explainable by other data. It was suspected that larger organizations would pay more than smaller ones for similar jobs due to the effects of such environmental factors as unionization, levels of technology, etc. Yet, as Table 4.11 shows, this was not the case.

Table 4.11: Hourly Rate of Pay

Category	Rate/Hour
1	$3.50**
2	3.49**
3	3.52 (N.S.)
4	3.33*
5	3.69**
6	3.24
7	3.20
8	3.27
9	3.14
10	3.36

*$p < .05$
**$p < .01$

Hourly rates are significantly higher in smaller organizations than in larger. This relationship remains significant when either skilled or unskilled employees are compared across size. It seems reasonable to assume that given similar skill levels, those individuals being compensated at a higher rate will be more satisfied with economic factors (particularly when promotions are not considered economic) than those being paid less. This was, indeed, found to be the case, as shown by the small section of Table 4.8 reconstructed here.[14]

Category	Pay	Benefits	Total
1	4.82**	5.27 (N.S.)	5.04**
2	4.89 (N.S.)	5.02 (N.S.)	4.95 (N.S.)
3	4.66**	5.82**	5.23**
4	4.79**	5.21 (N.S.)	4.99*
5	4.86**	5.34 (N.S.)	5.09**
6	4.05	5.10	4.57
7	4.52	4.95	4.73
8	3.72	5.21	4.45
9	4.07	5.11	4.59
10	4.03	5.08	4.54

*$p < .05$
**$p < .001$

As seen by the above table, monetary compensation is not the only concern of employees in what has been defined as the 'economic' area of the job. Fringe benefits also play an important role. While the above table indicates no significant differences in satisfaction levels across the categories, the table below shows that in terms of the amount of benefits offered, large organizations are more attractive than small. Employees were questioned concerning whether or not their employers or union provided any or all of ten different benefits.[15] Figures in the table below represent the average number of benefits given to employees in each category (Range = 0 - 10).

Table 4.12: Benefits Offered

Category	Number of Benefits
1	4.9**
2	4.5**
3	7.6 (N.S.)
4	4.0**
5	5.4*
6	6.8
7	6.1
8	8.2
9	7.2
10	6.5

*$p < .01$
**$p < .001$

This difference in the amount of benefits given may somewhat offset the affects of higher take home pay in smaller organizations. This point will be addressed in the following chapter. It is interesting to note at this point that the lack of a significant difference in satisfaction with benefits is in spite of the fact that more benefits are given in larger organizations. When benefits and longevity were correlated, the result was a coefficient of $+.320$ ($P < .001$), indicating that the amount of benefits is related to employee stability. The lack of a significant difference concerning satisfaction with benefits across size, coupled with higher pay levels and resultant higher satisfaction levels with pay in smaller organizations explains the finding of higher overall economic satisfaction among members of smaller organizations. In addition, it partially explains the more favorable turnover and stability rates in larger organizations, found despite the lesser amounts of satisfaction.

There remains, however, the question of individual value systems and the importance any particular group or individual attaches to the various sources of job satisfaction. It can be expected that the more importance attached to any particular source or group of sources of job satisfaction, the greater the effect of such source(s) on overall satisfaction levels and on resultant absenteeism or turnover/stability rates. The closer the match between the importance of the source(s) and the amount of satisfaction derived from those source(s) the greater the impact, as stated above, on overall satisfaction, absenteeism, and/ or turnover/stability. With this consideration in mind, the responses of subjects asked the following three questions, already discussed in the Methodology Chapter, were analyzed:

Now would you try to think of a specific time when you were
especially <u>satisfied</u> with your present job, a time when you
felt especially <u>good</u> about your job. Can you think of such
a time? . . . Exactly what happened to make you feel good?
Who or what was mainly responsible for this event?

What <u>two</u> things about this job give you the <u>most pleasure</u>?
What <u>two</u> things make you <u>happiest</u> about your job here?

How did you come to work in the solid waste management
field? What made you decide to work in this field?

Responses were classified according to the Coders Manual (Appendix B),
and categorized as either economic, social, or task. Three index
numbers were then computed from the four responses of each subject,
indicating the number of these responses classified as economic, social,
and task (0, 1, 2, 3, 4). This process was repeated twice, once with
promotions, subordinates, and amount of work considered, and once without.
In the tables below,[16] the four figures in the numerator represent the
number of responses falling in that particular category for the above
three questions. They are listed in the order presented above. The
reader is reminded that the possible range is 0-4.

Table 4.13: Individual Value Systems: Orientations Toward Work
(All Responses)

Category	Economic	Social	Task	Social and Task
1	$\frac{127 + 87 + 97 + 104}{379}$ = 1.095 (N.S.)	$\frac{85 + 106 + 133 + 32}{379}$ = .939 (N.S.)	$\frac{68 + 87 + 57 + 31}{379}$ = .644**	$\frac{154 + 193 + 190 + 63}{379}$ = 1.583 (N.S.)
2	$\frac{97 + 58 + 62 + 76}{264}$ = 1.110**	$\frac{48 + 65 + 103 + 26}{264}$ = .917**	$\frac{47 + 68 + 41 + 28}{264}$ = .697**	$\frac{95 + 133 + 144 + 54}{264}$ = 1.614 (N.S.)
3	$\frac{30 + 29 + 35 + 28}{115}$ = 1.061**	$\frac{37 + 41 + 30 + 6}{115}$ = .991*	$\frac{22 + 19 + 16 + 3}{115}$ = .522 (N.S.)	$\frac{59 + 60 + 46 + 9}{115}$ = 1.513 (N.S.)
4	$\frac{73 + 47 + 59 + 52}{186}$ = 1.242*	$\frac{38 + 43 + 62 + 8}{186}$ = .812*	$\frac{36 + 40 + 26 + 11}{186}$ = .608**	$\frac{74 + 83 + 88 + 19}{186}$ = 1.419*
5	$\frac{54 + 40 + 38 + 52}{193}$ = .953 (N.S.)	$\frac{47 + 63 + 71 + 24}{193}$ = 1.062 (N.S.)	$\frac{33 + 47 + 31 + 20}{193}$ = .679 (N.S.)	$\frac{80 + 110 + 102 + 44}{193}$ = 1.741 (N.S.)
6	$\frac{47 + 29 + 28 + 26}{119}$ = 1.092	$\frac{20 + 34 + 43 + 19}{119}$ = .975	$\frac{21 + 19 + 17 + 7}{119}$ = .538	$\frac{41 + 53 + 60 + 26}{119}$ = 1.513
7	$\frac{22 + 6 + 9 + 7}{54}$ = .815	$\frac{10 + 20 + 20 + 8}{54}$ = 1.074	$\frac{8 + 9 + 5 + 6}{54}$ = .519	$\frac{18 + 29 + 25 + 14}{54}$ = 1.593
8	$\frac{25 + 23 + 19 + 19}{65}$ = 1.323	$\frac{10 + 14 + 23 + 11}{65}$ = .892	$\frac{13 + 10 + 12 + 1}{65}$ = .554	$\frac{23 + 24 + 35 + 12}{65}$ = 1.446
9	$\frac{27 + 19 + 18 + 15}{69}$ = 1.145	$\frac{11 + 21 + 22 + 8}{69}$ = .899	$\frac{13 + 7 + 6 + 2}{69}$ = .406	$\frac{24 + 28 + 28 + 10}{69}$ = 1.304
10	$\frac{20 + 10 + 10 + 1}{50}$ = 1.020	$\frac{9 + 13 + 21 + 11}{50}$ = 1.080	$\frac{8 + 12 + 11 + 5}{50}$ = .720	$\frac{17 + 25 + 32 + 16}{50}$ = 1.800

*$p < .05$
**$p < .01$

Table 4.14: Individual Value Systems: Orientations Toward Work (Without Promotions, Subordinates, Amount of Work)

Category	Economic	Social	Task	Social and Task
1	$\frac{102 + 87 + 94 + 104}{379} = 1.021*$	$\frac{84 + 103 + 130 + 32}{379} = .924$ (N.S.)	$\frac{48 + 73 + 44 + 31}{379} = .517**$	$\frac{133 + 176 + 174 + 63}{379} = 1.441$ (N.S.)
2	$\frac{80 + 58 + 60 + 76}{264} = 1.038$ (N.S.)	$\frac{48 + 64 + 100 + 26}{264} = .902**$	$\frac{33 + 57 + 33 + 28}{264} = .572**$	$\frac{81 + 121 + 133 + 54}{264} = 1.474$ (N.S.)
3	$\frac{22 + 29 + 34 + 28}{115} = .983**$	$\frac{37 + 39 + 30 + 6}{115} = .974$ (N.S.)	$\frac{15 + 16 + 11 + 3}{115} = .391$ (N.S.)	$\frac{52 + 55 + 41 + 9}{115} = 1.365$ (N.S.)
4	$\frac{66 + 47 + 58 + 52}{186} = 1.199*$	$\frac{38 + 43 + 61 + 8}{186} = .807*$	$\frac{26 + 32 + 19 + 11}{186} = .473**$	$\frac{64 + 75 + 80 + 19}{186} = 1.280$ (N.S.)
5	$\frac{36 + 40 + 36 + 52}{193} = .850$ (N.S.)	$\frac{47 + 60 + 69 + 24}{193} = 1.036$ (N.S.)	$\frac{22 + 41 + 25 + 20}{193} = .560*$	$\frac{69 + 101 + 94 + 44}{193} = 1.596$ (N.S.)
6	$\frac{31 + 29 + 27 + 26}{119} = .950$	$\frac{20 + 34 + 42 + 19}{119} = .966$	$\frac{15 + 15 + 15 + 7}{119} = .437$	$\frac{35 + 49 + 57 + 26}{119} = 1.403$
7	$\frac{18 + 6 + 9 + 7}{54} = .741$	$\frac{10 + 20 + 19 + 8}{54} = 1.056$	$\frac{5 + 8 + 5 + 6}{54} = .444$	$\frac{15 + 28 + 24 + 14}{54} = 1.500$
8	$\frac{13 + 23 + 18 + 19}{65} = 1.123$	$\frac{10 + 14 + 23 + 11}{65} = .892$	$\frac{10 + 7 + 10 + 1}{65} = .431$	$\frac{20 + 21 + 33 + 12}{65} = 1.323$
9	$\frac{22 + 19 + 18 + 15}{69} = 1.073$	$\frac{11 + 21 + 22 + 8}{69} = .899$	$\frac{8 + 6 + 5 + 2}{69} = .304$	$\frac{19 + 27 + 27 + 10}{69} = 1.203$
10	$\frac{9 + 10 + 9 + 11}{50} = .780$	$\frac{9 + 13 + 20 + 11}{50} = 1.060$	$\frac{7 + 9 + 10 + 5}{50} = .670$	$\frac{16 + 22 + 30 + 16}{50} = 1.680$

*p < .05
**p < .01

As can be seen, task sources are the ones where the greatest difference is evident between those in large and small organizations, with those in the latter type placing a greater value on this aspect of employment. This is particularly true where all responses are categorized. The fact that those in smaller organizations are more satisfied with task aspects of the job (Table 4.8), coupled with the greater importance they attach to it, increases their level of overall satisfaction.

With the exception of economic aspects other than promotions, there is no other sifnificant difference across size in terms of value systems. Those in smaller organizations placed a greater value on economic considerations (less promotions), were paid more (Table 4.11), and were, thus, more satisfied with economic aspects of the job (Table 4.8). This finding holds despite the fact that those in large organizations had more comprehensive benefit packages (Table 4.12). As in the case of the task aspects, these economic factors also contribute to the higher overall job satisfaction found in smaller organizations (Tables 4.8 and 4.9).

Reading across Tables 4.13 and 4.14, it is evident that the subjects placed a much higher value on economic rewards than either social or task, and that the task aspects of the job were the least important of the three. Thus, it can be expected that economic sources are the single most important group contributing to overall satisfaction. The author mentions this in an attempt to reemphasize his earlier point, that a more realistic degree of emphasis concerning economic sources should be incorporated into present job satisfaction research.

In conclusion, then, the statistical analysis of the data supports one of the original hypotheses and fails to support the other. As regards absenteeism, it is seen to be negatively correlated with the amount of satisfaction from task sources. Satisfaction from these sources is found to be higher in smaller organizations, and absenteeism is, as hypothesized, thus, positively correlated with size. This is not exactly what the author expected to find, since the same relationship was also expected when social sources were considered, yet satisfaction from these sources remained constant across size. Looking at economic sources, those in smaller organizations expressed more satisfaction than employees in larger companies, the opposite of what was expected.

Turning to overall satisfaction, it is seen not to be the same across the size variable, but rather to be higher in smaller organizations. This is due to the combined effects of higher satisfaction levels with economic and task sources in smaller organizations and the lack of a difference for social sources. Despite this fact, those in larger organizations have lower projected turnover and higher stability than their counterparts in smaller concerns. This is further complicated by the fact that a low correlation is found between overall satisfaction and turnover and stability across subjects. This finding, i.e., that those in smaller organizations are more satisfied, yet have higher turnover and lower stability, make it obvious that the second hypothesis (same overall satisfaction, same turnover across size) is not supported. Reasons are detailed in the concluding chapter.

Footnotes

[1]See page 1 of Introduction for a definition of "orientation toward work".

[2]Economic rewards were not expected to affect feelings of attachment.

[3]The implicit assumption here is that orientation toward work will not, in the aggregate, vary across employees of different sized organizations.

[4]Small < 75, Large $\geq$ 76.

[5]For statistical significance, unless otherwise noted:
For dichotomous responses:
$H_o: P_1 = P_2$

$H_1: P_1 > P_2$

$$Z = \frac{\hat{P}_1 - \hat{P}_2}{S(\hat{P}_1 - \hat{P}_2)} = \frac{\hat{P}_1 - \hat{P}_2}{\sqrt{pq\,[(\frac{1}{n_1}) + (\frac{1}{n_2})]}}$$

This approximates, in fact, serves as the basis for the formula for practical significance.
For discrete responses:
$H_o: u_1 - u_2 = 0$

$H_1: u_1 - u_2 < 0$

$$T = \frac{\bar{X}_1 - \bar{X}_2}{Sp\sqrt{\frac{1}{n_1} + \frac{1}{n_2}}}$$

$$Sp = \frac{(n_1-1)S_1^2 + (n_2-1)S_2^2]\ 1/2}{n_1 + n_2 - 2}$$

$V = n_1 + n_2 - 2$

[6]Figures do not add to 100% due to those who intended to stay until retirement, but will retire in less than 5 years.

[7]Stability Rate = $\dfrac{\text{Number of Workers with Over 5 Years Service}}{\text{Number of Respondents within the Size Classification}}$

[8]See Appendix A, question 24a, and Appendix B, coding columns 33-34.

[9]See Chapter III for a complete listing and discussion of these questions. Also, see Appendix A for a listing of the questions.

[10]See the discussion preceding Table 4.2 of this chapter for an explanation of the 25 day cut-off.

[11] See Chapter V for a further discussion of this point.

[12] See discussion, page 68 for explanation of positive coefficient.

[13] Figures in body of table represent average response on a scale of 1 (extremely dissatisfied) to 7 (extremely satisfied).

[14] Medical, sick leave with pay, paid holidays, paid vacations or annual leave, retirement plan, group life insurance, profit sharing, workmens compensation, a credit union, or any other benefits not mentioned.

[15] Table 4.13

> Economic (Benefits, Money, Promotions)
> Social (Supervisors, Subordinates, Co-Workers)
> Task (Amount of Work, Variety in Work, Work Itself)
> 1st figures = number of economic, social, or task responses given to the question concerning a time when the employees felt especially satisfied with their jobs.
> 2nd & 3rd figures = number of economic, social, or task responses given to the question concerning the two things about the job giving the most pleasure.
> 4th figure = number of economic, social, or task responses given to the question concerning how the employee came to work in the field.

Table 4.14

> Economic (Benefits, Money)
> Social (Supervisors, Co-Workers)
> Task (Variety in Work, Work Itself)
> Figures are presented representing responses to the same ordering of questions as Table 4.13.

V CONCLUSIONS AND IMPLICATIONS

This book is intended to be a discussion of an empirical investigation of the 'size-effect' phenomenon among lower level employees in industrial organizations. Although Ingham[1] is the only author cited who uses the term 'size-effect', chapter II showed evidence of other researchers who have looked into the same problem. The present work is unlike most of those before it, in that it differentiates between the two most often used measures of withdrawal, absenteeism and turnover. Likewise, its findings are different than most, including Ingham's, in that they show both measures of withdrawal to be related to organization size, but in opposite directions.

Before elaborating on this point, the author wishes to restate the original hypotheses, with the intent of centering the discussion to follow around them. These hypotheses were as follows:

1. H_o: Quality of ⟵—— different than ——⟶ Quality of
   Satisfaction   Satisfaction
   (Sources)   (Sources)
   Larger   Smaller
   Organizations   Organizations

   Sources of Satisfaction = Economic
       Larger Organizations

   Sources = Social and task ——⟶ lead to ——⟶ Feelings of identity with
   of   and commitment to the
   Satisfaction   organization
   Smaller organizations

   Therefore:

   H_o: Absenteeism   >   Absenteeism
        Larger organizations   Smaller organizations

2. H_o: Quantity of Satisfaction = Quantity of Satisfaction
   Larger organizations   Smaller organizations

Therefore:

H_o: Turnover = Turnover
   Larger organizations   Smaller organizations

As regards the sources of satisfaction, the combination of satisfaction from social and task sources was, indeed, found to a greater extent in smaller organizations than larger (see Table 4.8). Yet, upon a closer inspection of the data, it is evident that this difference is due entirely to differences in satisfaction from task sources, as there is no significant difference between groups when satisfaction from social sources is isolated. Thus, it was the type, amount, and variety of the work that was more appealing in smaller organizations, a finding similar to those of Talacchi,[2] and Thomas and Fink[3] among others. The findings of Weber,[4] Terrien and Mills[5] and Hall, Haas, and Johnson[6] are also significant here for explanatory purposes. If, as they allege, increases in organization size cause more formalization throughout the organization and a narrower range of tasks within lower level jobs, and if workers are generally less satisfied with such a situation, as Hewitt and Parfit[7] and Indik[8] suggest, then the findings of the present study of less satisfaction from task sources in larger organizations is consistent with this prior research.

Additionally, the value systems of individuals in various size organizations bear the same relationship to each other as do the satisfaction measures in this area. Those in smaller organizations do not attach more importance to the combined social and task aspects of the job than do those employed in larger organizations. Closer analysis reveals no significant difference between the groups when social aspects are isolated, yet does identify the task functions as a source of differentiation (see Table 4.13 and 4.14). In summary, then, the author finds the value systems of the employees to be compatible with the rewards offered by the organization as regards task aspects in smaller organizations, and, thus, the finding of higher satisfaction levels in this area is the logical result.

In the area of economic considerations, the author's original belief was that employees in larger organizations would place a greater value on, and be more satisfied with, these aspects of the job than would their counterparts in smaller concerns. This turned out not to be the case. There was no significant difference between the importance either group attached to economic aspects of the job when pay, benefits, and promotions were all considered (Table 4.13). Yet, when only pay and benefits were analyzed, members of smaller organizations placed more value on this newly defined "economic" sector than those in larger organizations (Table 4.14). This evidence, coupled with the fact that those in smaller organizations are paid significantly more than those in larger concerns at similar skill levels (Table 4.11) leads to the conclusion that employees in smaller firms should be more satisfied with economic aspects of the job than those in larger.[9] This is, indeed, the case, as shown by Table 4.8,[10] and is counter to the original hypothesis.

Since those in smaller organizations are more satisfied than those in larger with task and economic sources and there is no significant difference regarding social aspects, one would expect overall satisfaction levels to be higher in smaller organizations. Findings of the present study offer evidence that this is, indeed, the case. Responses to both the 'faces' questions (Table 4.8) and the general question concerning occupational choice if given a chance to relive their lives

(Table 4.9), indicate that those in smaller organizations experience more overall job satisfaction. The author originally expected to find no significant difference across sizes in levels of overall satisfaction. The fact that there is a difference causes results other than those hypothesized regarding turnover and stability rates.

As can be seen from the original hypothesis, the author expected those with higher satisfaction levels from social and/or task sources to exhibit lower absenteeism rates. Tables 4.6 and 4.7 show a statistically significant negative relationship in all four correlations of satisfaction from social and task sources combined and absenteeism rates, thus supporting the original hypothesis. Once again, however, the degree of relationship is attributable almost exclusively to satisfaction from task sources.

Logically, then, if employees in smaller organizations are more satisfied with the task aspects of their jobs, and if this is, in turn, related to absenteeism rates, to be internally consistent the present data should reveal such absenteeism rates to be lower in smaller organizations. Correlation coefficients of +.182, +.289, and +.187 ($p < .001$) for the entire sample, the adjusted sample, and the point biserial tests, respectively, plus the results in Table 4.2, all show this to be the case.

As stated earlier in this chapter, the results regarding economic aspects of the job and their relationship to the size factor, were not what the author had expected. Those in smaller organizations placed more value on economic factors (excluding promotions) and received a higher rate of renumeration for their services. Thus, satisfaction from economic sources was negatively related to size. There was originally expected to be a positive relationship between these factors, and this was to balance out the higher satisfaction from social/task sources found in smaller organizations, thus causing <u>overall</u> satisfaction levels to remain constant across size. Since this was not the case, overall satisfaction levels were significantly higher among employees of smaller organizations. It seems logical to expect that less satisfied employees will not stay as long with their present employer as those who are more satisfied. This connection between longevity/turnover and overall satisfaction levels was not found in the present study, however. Those in larger organizations, with lower levels of overall satisfaction, actually had been employed longer in the past (Table 4.5) and intended to be employed longer in the future (Tables 4.3 and 4.4) with their present organization, than their more satisfied counterparts in smaller concerns. Correlation coefficients of .231 and .066 were found between size, and longevity and projected turnover,[11] respectively.

In other words, those in larger organizations were less satisfied with their jobs overall, yet had been there longer, and intended to remain in the same position longer, than their more satisfied counterparts in smaller organizations.

At this point, much of the information previously presented as well as one of the main findings of the study can best be summarized by a few first order partial correlation coefficients, as presented below:

<u>Talbe 5.1</u>: Partial Correlations

Variable	Correlated With Variable	Holding Constant	Coefficient
Size	Absenteeism	Satisfaction	+.0325 (N.S.)
Satisfaction	Absenteeism	Size	-.1078*
Size	Longevity	Satisfaction	+.2854**
Satisfaction	Longevity	Size	+.1149*

*p < .005
**p < .001

These partial correlation coefficients reveal, as the author has stated previously, that satisfaction is the key variable relating to absenteeism, with size acting as an intervening variable. The results regarding longevity appear at first to be inconsistent when coupled with the negative relationship between size and satisfaction. If these two variables are negatively related, as shown previously, what explains these positive partial coefficients when correlated with longevity? The author feels the situation is caused by a variable not considered in these partial correlations, that of non-monetary compensation, i.e., the benefit package. This factor will be dealt with in the following pages.

As regards the first hypothesis concerning variance in social and/or task sources of satisfaction and resulting absenteeism levels, the author's original expectations have been borne out concerning the task area. Economic satisfaction levels were the opposite of what was expected, and caused the second hypothesis concerning overall satisfaction not to be supported. All these findings can be explained by use of present data. Yet, the lack of relationship between overall satisfaction and turnover/stability, particularly in larger organizations cannot be.

The author believes there is more than one factor contributing to the existing situation regarding both turnover and stability. Looking at the satisfaction turnover/stability correlations reveals that something in the large sector is causing reduced turnover despite lower satisfaction. It was at first felt that the absolute level of monetary compensation in large firms relative to small would be an explanatory variable, but Table 4.11 shows this not to be the case.

Ingham, in his work, found an inverse relationship between turnover/ stability factors and overall job satisfaction.[12] Yet, he considered as a source of economic and overall satisfaction, "security of employment," a source not included in the 'faces questions' of the present study. It is the author's opinion that if the same classification had been used in both studies similar results would have been obtained in this area, as they were regarding absenteeism. The fact that less satisfied workers have higher stability and lower turnover in larger organizations may be partially attributable to the security factor not measured here. This seems to the author to be one likely explanation for the findings of the present work, particularly in light of the assertion of Hellriegel and Slocum[13] and Poidevin[14] that job security gains in importance as a factor of employment as one moves lower in the organization structure, and the authors belief that this security is more prevalent in larger firms due to labor organizations, formalized work rules, stated discipline and dismissal policies, etc.

Another factor the author believes contributes to the present findings is the type of work being done by the subjects of this study. They do not work within the physical facilities of their employers: they are out on the road in small work crews for almost the entire working day. Under these conditions, dissatisfaction with bureaucratization and formulization, a problem in larger concerns, will not be as likely to result in turnover as would otherwise be the case, since the employee can 'escape' some of the social and task conditions causing dissatisfaction. Since the present study differs markedly from Inghams regarding findings in this area, it is important to note that Ingham's subjects had jobs that kept them inside the physical facilities of their employer.

The difference in the benefit package across size is a third factor the author feels is important for explanatory purposes and for its contribution to the difference in findings between the present work and those of previous researchers who did not include the benefit package. While the present study shows no difference across size in terms of satisfaction with the benefit program, (Table 4.8), the additional benefits given in larger organizations (Table 4.12), particularly those with vesting provisions, may, indeed, cause employees in these larger organizations to stay longer, as evidenced by the +.320 ($p < .001$) correlation between benefits and longevity. This is true even though they are less satisfied than their counterparts in smaller firms, and explains the apparent contradiction in the partial correlations of Table 5.1. Even with their lower levels of satisfaction, those in larger organizations are willing to stay longer because of the additional benefits offered, perhaps reasoning that they will be giving up too much in the way of present and accumulated non-monetary compensation (benefits) if they leave. This feeling will of course be compounded the longer the individual stays with the firm.

It is this last factor that the author considers the most important in explaining the present findings regarding turnover/stability. When it is combined with the previously discussed factors of job security and location of job performance, the three present what the author feels is a strong explanatory base.

As regards the moderating effect of the ownership and skill level variables, the major differences uncovered in this study seem to center around the skilled (categories 5 and 10) and unskilled (categories 4 and 9) breakout. Unskilled workers are absent more and are less satisfied overall with the task aspects of their job than their skilled counterparts. Since the number of skilled and unskilled employees is proportionately the same across size its effect on the size breakout will be negligible. The relationship between satisfaction and absenteeism is consistent with that found across size. The same can be said regarding stability. Skilled employees were significantly more stable than their unskilled counterparts, yet expressed no more satisfaction with social or economic aspects of the job. This is despite the fact that they were paid significantly more and benefits were approximately the same. A look at their value system shows skilled employees to be more concerned with task aspects of the job and less concerned with economic aspects than their unskilled counterparts. Here again, the author would point out that the relationship of various factors is consistent with that found when size was the independent variable. Hence, it seems that results across skill levels, at least for the two classifications considered here, are supportive of the findings regarding size.

As regards the public versus private breakout the results are at best inconclusive. Those in public organizations are absent more, perhaps due to the firms providing a greater number of paid 'sick days', yet have a higher stability rate than those in privately owned concerns. In small organizations, the sample contained over twice as many employees of private, as opposed to public, organizations, while in the large sector the numbers were not significantly different. Thus, in the small sector of the sample, type of ownership was not supportive of the overall results.

In summary, then, the first set of hypotheses concerning absenteeism was supported by the data, the second concerning stability/turnover were not. The author wishes to point out that this is one of very few size-absenteeism studies in American industry.[15] The sample used here compares very favorably not only with those used in studies in this country, but with those used in Great Britain and France[16] as well. This favorable comparison includes the factors of overall sample size, variety of measurement, range of organization size, and geographic coverage.

Even with such a sample, however, this study dealt with only one aspect of the 'size-effect' phenomenon. Questions of strike activity, productivity levels, accidents, and organization structure, as related to size, have not been addressed statistically. Hopefully, future research will concentrate on some or all of these areas and thus provide behavioralists with a better understanding of the moderating effect of these variables in the size-satisfaction relationship. This research is needed in both the industrial and business sectors. In both sectors, other occupations need to be studied, not only individually, but in a cross-sectional manner, and the results compared. Future research is also needed to ascertain employees conceptualizations of promotions, amount of work, and relations with subordinates, i.e., whether or not they consider them economic, task, and/or social sources of satisfaction.

Additionally, research similar to that undertaken for the present study needs to be done with job security as an economic factor, and the results compared to the present study and Ingham's to determine the amount of influence this factor asserts. The effect of non-monetary benefits needs to be looked at more carefully to ascertain their impact on factors of satisfaction and turnover/stability rates. This should be done as a separate study, since the present work indicates it warrants independent investigation. The effects of other factors, such as age, education, and race, should also be studied and related to the dependent variables used here.[17]

Results of the research here indicate that smaller industrial organizations need to concentrate on providing a feeling of job security in their employees, probably best done through the benefit package, if they hope to reduce turnover levels and increase labor stability. Evidence indicates that they are presently doing an adequate job in economic and task aspects of the job relative to larger organizations, yet their turnover problems will remain until this 'security' is somehow incorporated into the compensation/benefit package.

Larger industrial organizations, while not faced with turnover problems to the same extent, should also see suggestions for improvement in the present study. Less satisfied workers can lead to numerous labor problems other than turnover rates.[18] It is possible that in their desire to achieve greater efficiency by breaking the job into its smallest increments, they have taken from the individual employee the opportunity to realize satisfaction from task sources. Limited programs of job enlargement or enrichment may serve to increase employee satisfaction from task sources in these larger organizations and, thus reduce some of the resultant problems. Data of the present study indicates that this may be particularly true in the case of absenteeism rates. Given the correlation betwen job satisfaction from task sources and absenteeism, if larger organizations can move closer to the position of their smaller counterparts as regards satisfaction with the work itself, variety in the work, and possibly the amount of work, their absenteeism rates can be expected to decrease. One of the most beneficial contributions a future researcher could make in this area would be to find large and/or small organizations that have attempted to move in the direction(s) indicated and conduct a longitudinal study to see if the above-mentioned changes do, in fact, begin to take place.

Thus, in conclusion, the author hopes that the present study will serve as a forerunner for future research in this country in the 'size-effect' area, and that the results arrived at herein will provide some degree of understanding and insight for behavioralists studying the most complex element in industrial organizations--the individual worker.

Footnotes

[1] Ingham, G. K., Size of Industrial Organization and Worker Behaviour, Cambridge University Press, 1970. The term was originally used by Durkheim; Durkheim, Emily, The Division of Labor in Society, Glencoe, Ill., 1933, pg. 356.

[2] Talacchi, S., "Organizational Size, Individual Attitudes, and Behavior: An Empirical Study", Administrative Science Quarterly, Volume 5, 1960.

[3] Thomas, E. J., and Fink, C. F., "Effects of Group Size", Psychological Bulletin, Volume 60, 1963.

[4] Weber, M., The Theory of Social and Economic Organization, New York: The Free Press, 1947.

[5] Terrien, F., and Mills, D., "The Effect of Changing Size Upon the Internal Structure of Organizations", American Sociological Review, Volume 20, 1955.

[6] Hall, R. F., Haas, J. E., and Johnson, N. H., "Organization Size, Complexity, and Formalization", American Sociological Review, Volume 32, 1967.

[7] Hewitt, D., and Parfit, J., "A Note on Working Morale and Size of Group", Occupational Psychology, Volume 27, 1953.

[8] Indik, B. P., "Some Effects of Organization Size on Member Attitudes and Behavior", Human Relations, Volume 16, 1963.

[9] This finding holds true despite the greater amount of benefits offered in larger organizations, since the discussion here concerns satisfaction, and this was found not to be different across size concerning benefits.

[10] Although the specific point is not of direct concern for this study, the author suggests the reader compare the relative levels of importance attached by employees in all categories to economic, social and task aspects of the job. It is readily apparent that monetary compensation is still far and away the single most important aspect of the job for all employees. This reaffirms the author's personal belief that the orientation of lower level employees is basically economistic, that monetary compensation is the biggest single source of power in industrial organizations, and that recent behavioral research has overemphasized the non-economic aspect of the job, particularly for lower level employees.

[11] The positive nature of the size-turnover coefficient is explained in the preceding chapter.

[12] Ingham, G.K., Size of Industrial Organization and Worker Behavior, Cambridge University Press, 1970, pg. 24.

[13] Hellriegel, D., and Slocum, J. W., Management: A Contingency Approach, Addison-Wesley, 1974.

[14] Poidevin, S. L., "A Study of Factors Affecting Labor Turnover", Personnel Practice Bulletin, Volume 1, 1949.

[15] Ingham, G. K., Size of Industrial Organization and Worker Behaviour, Cambridge University Press, 1970, pg. 150.

[16] Zurcher, L. A., Meadows, A., and Zurcher, S. L., "Value Orientation, Role Conflict, and Alientation from Work: A Cross Cultural Study", American Sociological Review, Volume 30, 1965, pp. 539-548.

[17] In the present study, age was found not to be significant different across size, education was significant higher in four of the five comparisons for employees in smaller organizations, and a racial breakout revealed significantly more whites in smaller organizations and blacks in larger, as well as the fact that in relation to their percent of the total population blacks comprise a disproportionately high number of employees in this occupation.

Category	Age	Education in Years	% White	Race % Black	% Other
1	34.7 (N.S.)	10.7**	68.3**	30.2*	1.5
2	31.2*	11.3**	63.6 (N.S.)	34.5 (N.S.)	1.9
3	39.1 (N.S.)	9.5 (N.S.)	78.2**	21.1**	.7
4	31.4**	10.2*	59.7*	39.5 (N.S.)	.8
5	37.1*	10.9*	77.0*	20.9 (N.S.)	2.1
6	35.7	9.2	57.1	36.7	6.2
7	33.2	8.5	61.3	33.9	4.8
8	38.5	10.1	54.1	38.8	7.1
9	38.2	8.9	48.8	46.4	4.8
10	33.3	9.5	68.3	23.8	7.9

*p < .01
**p < .001

[18] Bachman, J. G., Smith, C. G., and Slesinger, J. A., "Control, Performance, and Satisfaction: An Analysis of Structural and Individual Effects", Journal of Personality and Social Psychology, Volume 4, 1966; Sexton, W. P., "Organizational and Industrial Needs: A Conflict?", Personnel Journal, Volume 46, 1967.

APPENDIX A

OMB#
158-S71016

1-
2- _____ Interviewer: Do NOT Fill In _____
3-
4-
5-

Study Code No.   Interview Code No.

EMPLOYEE QUESTIONNAIRE (Refuse)

Date: _____

6-
Name of Interviewer: _____

Name of Organization: _____

7-
Size of Organization: _____   8-

Tele. No.: _____ SMSA or County Code _____
                        Region _____

(INTERVIEWER: GET THE INFORMATION THAT FOLLOWS (A-G) ON THIS PAGE BEFORE BEGINNING THE RESPONDENT'S INTERVIEW)

A. Type of Organization (CHECK ONE):

Private	( )	9-1
City	( )	-2
County	( )	-3
State	( )	-4
Federal	( )	-5

B. Name of Respondent (PRINT): _____
                                 last   first

C. Job Level (CHECK ONE):

Unskilled	( )	10-1
Skilled	( )	-2
Foreman/Supervisor	( )	-3
Secretarial/Clerical	( )	-4
Managerial/Technical/ Professional	( )	-5

D. Employee Code (CHECK ONE):

   W ( )   11-1
   B ( )   -2

E. No. of promotions since hiring (COUNT INCREASES IN RESPONSIBILITY, SKILL REQUIREMENTS, OR PRIVILEGES AS PROMOTIONS: PAY INCREASES AS SUCH DO NOT COUNT UNLESS ACCOMPANIED BY ONE OR MORE OF ABOVE). 12-
   _____

F. Working days absent in last month (last four working weeks.)
    (COUNT SICK LEAVE AND LEAVE WITHOUT PAY BUT NOT ANNUAL LEAVE)   13-
    _____ da.   14-

G. Working days absent in last six months (COUNT SICK LEAVE AND   15-
    LEAVE WITHOUT PAY BUT NOT ANNUAL LEAVE) _____ da.   16-

"GOOD MORNING (AFTERNOON). MY NAME IS _____.
I AM FROM APPLIED MANAGEMENT SCIENCES, A RESEARCH FIRM IN THE WASHINGTON, D.C. AREA. WE ARE WORKING ON A CONTRACT SUPPORTED BY THE FEDERAL GOVERNMENT TO STUDY ORGANIZATIONS AND EMPLOYEES IN THE SOLID WASTE MANAGEMENT FIELD. ONE OF THE THINGS WE WANT TO STUDY ARE THE ATTITUDES OF PEOPLE ALREADY WORKING IN THIS FIELD. WE WANT TO KNOW WHAT KIND OF THINGS THEY LIKE ABOUT THIS TYPE OF WORK, WHAT TYPE OF THINGS THEY DISLIKE, WHAT THEIR ATTITUDES ARE TOWARDS THE PERSONNEL POLICIES OF THEIR ORGANIZATION AND OTHER ASPECTS OF THEIR JOB. THIS INFORMATION MAY HELP ORGANIZATIONS IN THIS BUSINESS TO IMPROVE THEIR POLICIES AND PRACTICES.

"YOU ARE ONE OF SEVERAL HUNDRED EMPLOYEES ALL ACROSS THE COUNTRY THAT WILL BE INTERVIEWED FOR THIS PROJECT. YOUR NAME WAS DRAWN AT RANDOM FROM THE ORGANIZATION'S FILES.

"WE ASSURE YOU THAT EVERYTHING YOU TELL US WILL BE STRICTLY CONFIDENTIAL. YOUR ANSWERS WILL BE SEEN ONLY BY ME AND MY ASSOCIATES AT APPLIED MANAGEMENT SCIENCES. ONCE YOUR ANSWERS HAVE BEEN CODED AND STORED ON OUR COMPUTER, THIS QUESTIONNAIRE WILL BE DESTROYED SO THAT THERE WILL BE NO WAY TO IDENTIFY YOU.

"BEFORE WE BEGIN, DO YOU HAVE ANY QUESTIONS. . .?"

1. How long have you worked here? ___yrs. ___mos. 17-
 18-

2. How many different jobs did you have in the last five (5) years before coming here? _____ 19-

3. Are you a veteran?

        yes ( ) 20-1 (ASK Q. 3a)
        no ( )   -2 (SKIP TO Q. 4)

3a. How many years ago did you leave the armed forces?

                  21-
   _____ years 22-

4. How old were you on your last birthday? _____yrs. 23-
 24-

5. How many years of schooling have you completed? _____yrs. 25-
(WRITE IN TOTAL NUMBER OF YEARS, E.G., GRADE SCHOOL GRADUATE = 8; TWO YEARS OF HIGH SCHOOL = 10; HIGH SCHOOL GRADUATE = 12; JR. COLLEGE GRADUATE = 14; COLLEGE GRADUATE = 16; FOR M. A. DEGREE, ENTER 18; FOR Ph. D. ENTER 20, REGARDLESS OF ACTUAL YEARS OF GRADUATE SCHOOL).

6. Are you (READ LIST)

        married or   ( )   27-1
        single or   ( )   -2
        divorced or separated ( )   -3
        or
        a widow (widower)   ( )   -4

7. How many people depend on you for their major financial support?

        _____ 28-

8a. What is your job title, that is, what is your job called?

_____

8b. Can you tell me briefly, what your job duties are?

_____

_____

_____

8c. Which of these do you spend most of your time doing?

_____ 29-
                                        30-

8d. IF EMPLOYEE IS A BLUE COLLAR DOING COLLECTION, ASK:) On your usual route, is it mainly or solely curb service or mainly or solely non-curb service?

        mainly or solely curb service   ( ) 31-1
        mainly or solely non-curb service ( )   -2

9. Are you union or non-union?

        union   ( ) 32-1
        non-union ( )   -2

10. Who was the main person who told you how to do your work when you started your present job here, that is, who gave you your on-the-job training?

    No one   ( ) 33-1 (SKIP TO Q. 10b)
    A (more experienced) co-worker   ( )   -2
    A foreman, supervisor or other   ( )
        superior   -3
    Other (SPECIFY)   ( )   -4

_____

10a. How long did this on-the-job training last?

    one or less working days   ( ) 34-1 (SKIP TO Q. 10b)
    2 to 5 working days   ( )   -2
    6 to 10 working days   ( )   -3
    11 to 20 working days   ( )   -4
    more than 20 working days ( )   -5

10b. Did you receive any off-the-job training for your present job such as lectures, courses, films, demonstrations, or practice training with the regular equipment you would use on the job?

    yes ( ) 35-1
    no   ( )   -2 (SKIP TO Q. 10e)

10c. Who was the main person who did this off-the-job training?

    A (more experienced) co-worker ( ) 36-1
    A foreman, supervisor or other
        superior   ( )   -2
    An outside specialist or firm ( )   -3
    Other (SPECIFY)   ( )   -4

_____

10d. How long did this off-the-job training last?

one or less working days	( )	37-1
2 to 5 working days	( )	-2
6 to 10 working days	( )	-3
11 to 20 working days	( )	-4
more than 20 working days	( )	-5

(INTERVIEWER FILL IN; DO NOT ASK; SUM OF 10a + 10d CODES:_____) 38-
39-

10e. Do you have annual "refresher" training?

yes ( )   40-1 (ASK Q. 10f)
no ( )   -2 (SKIP TO Q. 11a)

10f. How long does it last?

one or less working days	( )	41-1
2 to 5 working days	( )	-2
6 to 10 working days	( )	-3
11 to 20 working days	( )	-4
more than 20 working days	( )	-5

11. a) How many days do you typically work per week? _____ da. 42-
    43-
    b) How many regular hours do you typically work per day? _____ hrs. 44-
    c) How many overtime hours do you typically work ___ hr. 45-
       per week (IF HOURLY)? 46-
       47-
    d) How many hours long is your typical work week? ___ hr. 48-
       (THIS SHOULD = a x b + c; CHECK FOR CONTRADICTIONS).
       49-
    e) What is your present hourly pay (IF HOURLY)? $_____ hr. 50-
       51-
    f) What is your overtime pay rate per hour? $ _____ hr. 52-
       (IF HOURLY)
       53-
    g) What is your present take home pay per week? $____ wk. 54-
    h) What is your present gross pay per week, that is,
       before deductions? $ _____ wk. 55-
       56-

12a. Have you had any promotions since you have been with the organization. . . (COUNT INCREASES IN RESPONSIBILITY, SKILL REQUIREMENTS OR PRIVILEGES AS PROMOTIONS; PAY INCREASES AS SUCH DO NOT COUNT UNLESS ACCOMPANIED BY ONE OR MORE OF ABOVE).

yes ( )   57-1
no ( )   -2

12b. (IF YES, ASK:) How many?

    _____58-   (CHECK FOR CONTRADICTIONS
                                  WITH COVER PAGE)   59-
    (No. of Promotions per year: _____) (INTERVIEWER: DO   60-
                                                   NOT FILL IN)

12c. How long ago was your last promotion?   61-
                                                                      62-

    _____yrs. _____mos.

13a. Have you had any pay raises since you have been with this organization?

    yes   ( )   63-1
    no   ( )   -2

13b. (IF YES, ASK:) How many?
        64-
    _____65-
                                                                    66-
    (No. of Pay Raises Per year: _____) (INTERVIEWER: DO 67-
                                                             NOT FILL IN)

13c. How long ago was your last pay raise?   68-
                                                               69-

    _____yrs. _____mos.

14. Do you get (have) (PLACE CHECK IN APPROPRIATE BOX)

(IF YES, ASK:) What part of the cost does your organization (or union) pay?

	yes	no	don't know	none	part	all
a) Medical/surgical benefits here?	( ) 70-1	( )-2	( )-3	( ) 71-1	( )-2	( )-3
b) Sick leave with pay?	( ) 72-1	( )-2	( )-3	X	X	X
c) Paid holidays (Xmas, etc.)?	( ) 73-1	( )-2	( )-3	X	X	X
d) Paid vacations or annual leave?	( ) 74-1	( )-2	( )-3	X	X	X
e) A retirement or pension plan?	( ) 75-1	( )-2	( )-3	( ) 76-1	( )-2	( )-3
f) Group life insurance?	( ) 77-1	( )-2	( )-3	( ) 78-1	( )-2	( )-3
g) Profit sharing? 80-1 CARD 2	( ) 79-1	( )-2	( )-3	X	X	X
h) Workmen's Compensation?	( ) 5-1	( )-2	( )-3	X	X	X
i) A credit union?	( ) 6-1	( )-2	( )-3	X	X	X
j) Any other benefits? (SPECIFY) _____	( ) 7-1					
k) _____	( ) 8-1					

(TOTAL # OF "YES'S" = ____)

9-
10-

CARD 2   Cols.

   1-
   2-
   3-
   4-

(Same as CARD 1)

15a. Now I am going to read a list of factors that may or may not have some effect on who gets ahead here. Tell me if each of the factors does or does not have an effect on who gets promoted here, based on your own experience.

	Q. 15a	Q. 15b Most Important	Q. 15c 2nd Most Important
( ) doing good work and being reliable about attendance	yes ( ) 11-1 no ( ) 11-2	( ) 19-1	( ) 20-1
( ) having pull, that is, political connections or being a personal friend of someone or being related to someone	yes ( ) 12-1 no ( ) 12-2	( ) -2	( ) -2
( ) having enough education	yes ( ) 13-1 no ( ) 13-2	( ) -3	( ) -3
( ) having seniority (no. of yrs. with organization)	yes ( ) 14-1 no ( ) 14-2	( ) -4	( ) -4
( ) having the right kind or amount of experience	yes ( ) 15-1 no ( ) 15-2	( ) -5	( ) -5
( ) being in a certain racial or ethnic group (which? _____)	yes ( ) 16-1 no ( ) 16-2	( ) -6	( ) -6
( ) passing a test or exam	yes ( ) 17-1 no ( ) 17-2	( ) -7	( ) -7
( ) are there any other? (SPECIFY) _____ _____	yes ( ) 18-1 no ( ) 18-2	( ) -8	( ) -8

15b. Now tell me which of these is most important in determining who gets ahead here based on your own experience. (READ EMPLOYEE THE FACTORS WHICH WERE CHECKED "YES" AND RECORD UNDER Q. 15b)

15c. (IF TWO FACTORS WERE CHECKED "YES", PLACE AN "X" UNDER Q. 15c NEXT TO THE OTHER FACTOR OR IF ONE WAS CHECKED SKIP TO Q. 16. IF MORE THAN TWO FACTORS WERE CHECKED "YES", READ THE QUESTION BELOW AND PLACE AN "X" UNDER Q. 15c BESIDE THE SECOND MOST IMPORTANT FACTOR). Now tell me which of these is next most important in determining who gets ahead here. (READ REMAINING FACTORS CHECKED "YES").

16. (SHOW EMPLOYEE CARD A). If a person doing a job like yours shows up for work regularly, works hard, and does good quality work, what are the chances that he will get ahead here? (READ CARD A ALTERNATIVES AND HAVE HIM CHOOSE ONE).

1 ( )		no chance	21-1
2 ( )			-2
3 ( )			-3
4 ( )			-4
5 ( )			-5
		certain	

17. What would you say your chances are of being promoted within the next:

    a) six months (if you stay here)? _____ 22- (READ CARD
    b) 12 months (if you stay here)? _____ 23- A ALTERNA-
    c) two years (if you stay here)? _____ 24- TIVES AND
    HAVE HIM
    CHOOSE ONE).

18. What is the best job you think you could ever get in this organization? _____

19. How many more times would you have to get promoted to get this (best) job? _____ 25-

20. Based on present pay rates, what is the most pay you think you could ever make here? _____ 26-
(TRANSLATE INTO GROSS PAY PER WEEK $ _____). 27-

21. What would you say your chances are of getting one or more pay raises within the next:

    a) six months (if you stay here)? _____ 28- (SHOW EMPLOYEE
    b) 12 months (if you stay here)? _____ 29- CARD A AGAIN,
    c) two years (if you stay here)? _____ 30- READ ALTERNATIVES
    AND HAVE HIM
    CHOOSE ONE).

22. How did you come to work for this organization, that is how did you get your job here? (CHECK ALTERNATIVE WHICH BEST FITS EMPLOYEE'S ANSWER).

    public employment agency (CITY, STATE, ETC.)   ( )   31-1
    private employment agency   ( )   -2
    advertisement (radio, TV, newspaper)   ( )   -3
    personal acquaintance, friend, or relative (or   ( )   -4
    friend of a friend)
    posted vacancy (bulletin board, etc.)   ( )   -5
    walk-in   ( )   -6
    appointed to job   ( )   -7
    other (SPECIFY) _____   ( )   -8

23. How did you come to work in the solid waste management field? What made you decide to work in this field? _____

    _____ 32-

24a. How much longer do you intend to work for this organization?
                                                        33-
          _____ yrs.   _____ mos.   34-

24b. Is this up to the age of retirement?

          yes ( ) 35-1
          no ( )   -2

25. Do you hope to be working in the solid waste management field (e.g., refuse, scrap) five (5) years from now?

          yes ( ) 36-1
          no ( )   -2

To answer these next few items, you will need to use this card. (HAND CARD B TO INTERVIEWEE). You can see that there are seven faces on the card. The faces go from a deep frown indicating extreme dissatisfaction (POINT TO FACE) to a deep smile indicating extreme satisfaction (POINT TO FACE). Under each face is a number. When I ask you, please tell me the number under the face which shows how satisfied or dissatisfied you are with the things I ask you about. Do not be afraid to express dissatisfaction if you really feel it. Remember, no one in this organization will ever see your answer. (EXPLAIN FURTHER IF NECESSARY; IF NUMBERS ARE CONFUSING, HAVE RESPONDENT POINT TO APPROPRIATE FACE).

26. You said that the actual work you do consists mainly of . . . (SEE Q. 8). Think about how you feel about the work itself, that is, if you find your work tasks interesting or boring, or too hard or too easy, if you like them or dislike them, etc. Tell me the

number of the face that shows how you feel about your present tasks.

_____ 37-

27. Do you have a supervisor. . .? Think about how you feel about your supervisor. Tell me the number of the face that shows how you feel about your supervisor.

_____ 38-

28. Do you work with people other than your supervisor, that is, with co-workers at the same level as yourself. . .? Think about how you feel about your co-workers in general. Tell me the number of the face that shows how you feel about your co-workers.

_____ 39-

29. Do you supervise or work with any subordinates, that is, people at a lower job level than you. . .? Tell me the number of the face that shows how satisfied or dissatisfied you are with the subordinates you work with.

_____ 40-

30. You said that the organization (or union) provides the following benefits. . . (SEE Q. 14, 1st COLUMN). Think about how satisfied or dissatisfied are you with these benefits. Tell me the number of the face that shows how you feel about the benefits you get here.

_____ 41-

31. Now let's consider your pay. You said that your present take home pay comes to about. . . a week (SEE Q. 11g). Tell me the no. of the face that shows how you feel.

_____ 42-

32. Now let's talk about promotions. You said that so far you have received. . . promotions (SEE Q. 12b) and think your chances of getting another within two years are. . .(SEE Q. 17c). Would you like more chances for promotion than you have now or are you satisfied with the way things are. . .? Tell me the number of the face that shows how you feel about your promotions opportunities here.

_____ 43-

33. Do you have any variety on this job, that is, do you have a chance to do many different kinds of things, or do you do the same thing every day. . .? Would you like more variety or are you satisfied with the amount you have now. . .? Tell me the number of the face that shows how you feel about the amount of variety on your job.

_____ 44-

34. How is the amount of work on your job on a typical day? Do you have just the right amount or do you have too much or too little to do. . .? Tell me the number of the face that shows how satisfied or dissatisfied you are with the amount of work you have on this job on a typical day.

_____ 45-

35. Tell me the number of the face that shows how satisfied or dissatisfied you are with each of the following:

   a) the equipment you use on your job. _____ 46-
   b) the hours of work. _____ 47-

   (ENTER SUM OF ITEMS 26 THROUGH 35; INTERVIEWER DO NOT COMPUTE) 48-
   49-

36. Now would you try to think of a specific time when you were especially satisfied with your present job, a time when you felt especially good about your job. Can you think of such a time? (IF NOT, PROBE). . . Exactly what happened to make you feel good? What led up to this good feeling? (BE SURE TO INDICATE BY UNDERLINING WHICH WAS THE SINGLE MOST IMPORTANT EVENT). Who or what was mainly responsible for this event? (RECORD AGENT RESPONSIBLE FOR MOST IMPORTANT EVENT). 50-
51-
52-

(ALTERNATE ORDER OF Q. 36 AND Q. 37)

37. Now would you try to think of a specific time when you were especially dissatisfied with your present job, a time when you felt especially bad about your job. Can you think of such a time? (IF NOT, PROBE). . . Exactly what happened to make you feel bad? 53-
What led up to this bad feeling? (BE SURE TO INDICATE BY UNDER- 54-
LINING WHICH WAS THE MOST IMPORTANT EVENT). Who or what was 55-
mainly responsible for this event? (RECORD AGENT RESPONSIBLE FOR MOST IMPORTANT EVENT).

(INTERVIEWER: CHECK HERE WHICH QUESTION YOU ASKED FIRST)

   Q. 36 ( )
   Q. 37 ( )

38. Have you ever experienced personally or witnessed (seen) any incident showing discrimination or prejudice on the part of some member of this organization. . .? (PROBE). . . Exactly what happened? Who was involved? When? (RECORD THE TYPE OF EVENT, THE PERSON RESPONSIBLE AND WHEN THE EVENT HAPPENED).

39. (SHOW EMPLOYEE CARD C). Would you recommend a career in the solid waste management field to a young person with your educational background who was just starting out ? (READ CARD C ALTERNATIVES AND HAVE HIM CHOOSE ONE).

    1 ( )   56-1
    2 ( )   -2
    3 ( )   -3
    4 ( )   -4
    5 ( )   -5

40. If you were starting over again in your work career, would you choose to work in the solid waste management field? (READ CARD C ALTERNATIVES AND HAVE HIM CHOOSE ONE).

    1 ( )   57-1
    2 ( )   -2
    3 ( )   -3
    4 ( )   -4
    5 ( )   -5

41. Now I would like you to think back to this morning (or any typical morning) when you were getting ready to come to work or were on your way to work. I would like to know what you were thinking about as you got ready to leave or as you were on your way. Can you remember this?. . . (GET CONTENT OF THOUGHT AND DIRECTION OF AFFECT). How did you feel? What kind of mood were you in?   58-
59-
60-

(READ PASSAGE BELOW BEFORE Q. 42 or Q. 43, WHICHEVER YOU ASK FIRST).
Now consider all aspects of your job: the work task you perform, your pay, your chances for promotion, the supervisors, co-workers and subordinates you have, the benefits you get, or any other aspect of the job you consider important:

42. What two things about this job give you the most pleasure? What two things make you happiest about your job here? (SPECIFY REASON OR EXPLAIN ANSWER).

    1. _____   61-
                                                        62-
                                                        63-
    2. _____   64-

(ALTERNATE ORDER OF Q. 42 AND Q. 43)

43. What two things about this job give you the most displeasure? What two things make you most unhappy about your job here?

43. (SPECIFY REASON OR EXPLAIN ANSWER).
    1. _____ 65-
                                                66-
                                                67-
    2. _____ 68-

INTERVIEWER: CHECK HERE WHICH QUESTION YOU ASKED FIRST)
                    Q. 42 ( )
                    Q. 43 ( )

44. If you had your life to live over, would you like to wind up in the same line of work as the one you're doing now?

                    yes ( ) 69-1
                    no ( )   -2

45. Do you know of any job that you could get right now (with your present skills and experience) that you would like better than this one?
    _____yes (What is it? _____) 70-
    _____no (CHECK ONE AND FILL IN AS APPROPRIATE)

    45a. (IF YES) "What stops you from taking such a job?"   71-

    45b. Do you know of any job you could get right now where the <u>pay</u> is better than here? _____yes (what is it? _____); _____no.   72-

    45c. (IF YES), "What stops you from taking such a job?"   73-

    45d. Do you know of any job you could get right now where the <u>chances for promotion</u> would be better than you have here? _____yes (what is it? _____);
    _____no   74-

    45e. (IF YES), "What stops you from taking such a job?"   75-

    45f. Do you know of any job you could get right now where the <u>work tasks</u> you would be doing would be more enjoyable than they are here? _____yes (what is it? _____); _____no.   76-

    45g. (IF YES), "What stops you from taking such a job?"   77-

    45h. Do you know of any job you could get right now where the <u>amount of work</u> you were given would be more to your liking than it is here? _____yes (what is it? _____); _____no.   78-

    45i. (IF YES), "What stops you from taking such a job?"   79-

46. Do you have a home telephone where you can be reached in case we have to contact you again? _____no; _____yes 80-2
    (No. ( ) _____)

APPENDIX B

CODERS' MANUAL FOR EMPLOYEE QUESTIONNAIRE (Refuse & SIC 5093)

GENERAL PRINCIPLES

The principles listed below are rules which will apply to the coding of the non-open ended items after the cover page on the quesionnaire. Memorizing these principles will help you to do the coding more rapidly and more accurately. (1) All of the codes that you will write will be numbers (with one exception which is given in #2 below). All the code numbers will go in the spaces or be circled to the rights of the column numbers which appear near the right hand margin of the questionnaire. Column numbers are to the left of all the dashes. (See Sample 1 below).

Sample 1

5. How many years of schooling have you completed? __10__ yrs.   25-1
   (WRITE IN TOTAL NUMBER OF YEARS, E.G., GRADE SCHOOL   26-0
   GRADUATE = 8; TWO YEARS OF HIGH SCHOOL = 10; HIGH SCHOOL
   GRADUATE = 12; JR. COLLEGE GRADUATE = 14; COLLEGE GRADUATE
   = 16; FOR M. A. DEGREE, ENTER 18; FOR Ph. D. ENTER 20,
   REGARDLESS OF ACTUAL YEARS OF GRADUATE SCHOOL).

6. Are you: (READ LIST)

   married or   ( ) 27-1
   single   ( )   -2
   divorced or separated or   ( )   -3
   a widow (widower)   ( )   -4

(2) All questions answered "NA" or left blank because they do not apply to the person in principle will not be coded. Questions coded "NA" because employee could not or would not answer are to be coded "X" or "XX" (depending on number of columns), except where "X" is used for other purposes. (See Sample 2 below).

Sample 2

	Not Coded
If yes, how many years ago did you leave the Armed Forces? __NA__ yrs.	21- 22-

(3) If a number is placed in an answer space on the questionnaire, this number itself or part of this number will be the code. More specific instructions are given below:

(a) If the number in the answer is <u>one</u> digit and one code column is provided, enter or circle the same number in the code space. Do the same for two digit answers and two code columns <u>providing</u> there are no mixed units such as yrs. and mos. or $ and ¢. (See Samples 3a & 3b below).

Samples 3a & 3b

	Code
How many days do you typically work per week? __5__ da.	42-5
How old were you on your last birthday? __36__ yrs.	23-3 24-6

(b) If the number in the answer is one digit and two code columns are provided, enter 0 in the first column and the number in the second column. (See Sample 4 following).

Sample 4

Working days absent in last month (last four working weeks). (COUNT SICK LEAVE AND LEAVE WITHOUT PAY BUT NOT ANNUAL LEAVE) __3__ da.	13-0 14-3

(c) If answer is in dollars and/or dollars and cents, the answer will have to be rounded. Round first <u>two</u> digits to nearest digit; if third number is a 5, round to nearest even number (e.g., $1.42 = 14; $2.48 = 25; $1.55 = 16; $2.25 = 22). If hourly amount is less than $1.00 or weekly amount is less than $100 enter 0 in 1st code. (See Samples 5a and 5b below).

Samples 5a & 5b

What is your present take home pay per week? $125.00wk.　53-1
　　　　　　　　　　　　　　　　　　　　　　　　　　　　　54-2
What is your present gross pay per week, that is,　　　　55-0
before deductions?　　　　　　　　　　　　$94.00 wk.　56-9

(d) If answer is in years and months, round to nearest year; if 6 mos. is entered, round to nearest _even_ year (e.g., 2 yrs., 3 mos. = 02; 12 yrs., 8 mos. = 13; 5 yrs., 6 mos. = 6; 10 yrs., 6 mos. = 10). (See Samples 6a & 6b below).

(if _only_ mos. are entered - 7 mo. or more = 1 yr.; 6 mos. or less = 0)

Samples 6a & 6b

How long have you worked here?　_12_ yrs.　_6_ mos.　17-1
　　　　　　　　　　　　　　　　　　　　　　　　　　　18-2

How long ago was your last promotion?　　　　　　　　　　61-0
　_2_ yrs.　_3_ mos.　　　　　　　　　　　　　　　　　　62-2

(4) If the answer on the questionnaire consists of a check mark (✓), the following simple coding principle applies: Circle the number to the right of the checked alternative. (See Sample 7 below).

Sample 7

How did you come to work for this organization, that is, how did you get your job here? (CHECK ALTERNATIVE WHICH BEST FITS EMPLOYEE'S ANSWER).

public employment agency (CITY, STATE, ETC.)　( ) 31-1
private employment agency　　　　　　　　　　　( )　-2

---

*If there are 2 code columns, remember 1st column = 0; see (b) above.

advertisement (radio, TV, newspaper)	( )	-3
personal acquaintance, friend, or relative (or friend of a friend)	( )	-4
posted vacancy (bulletin board, etc.)	( )	-5
walk-in	( )	-6
appointed to job	( )	-7

(5) If the question is open-ended (so that the answer consists of written words), a special coding system is provided for that question. These coding systems are shown in later pages of this appendix.

SPECIFIC CODING INSTRUCTIONS FOR EACH ITEM

While the above principles will make it possible to code all the non-open-ended items not on the cover page, specific instructions are given for each item below to insure that there will be no misunderstanding.

CARD 1

Column(s)	Item No.	Code
1, 2	Cover	Enter study code number
3, 4, 5	Cover	Enter number based on chronological receipt of questionnaire starting with 001, 002, 003, etc. Coordinate this with other coders.
6	Cover	Enter interviewer's code number based on page(s) 123
7 & 8	Cover	Enter code for company size from page(s) 124 after matching employee questionnaire with corresponding management questionnaire.
9	Cover, A	Circle no.: private = 1, city = 2, ... federal = 5
10	Cover, C	Circle no.: unskilled = 1, skilled = 2, ... managerial/professional = 5
11	Cover, D	See page(s) 132
12	Cover, E	Enter no. of promotions
13, 14	Cover, F	Enter no. of days absent; if less than 10, enter 0 in col. 13
15, 16	Cover, G	Same as cols. 13, 14
17, 18	1	Enter no. of yrs., rounded to nearest yr.; if 6 mos., round to nearest even yr.
19	2	Enter no. of jobs (if more than 10, enter 9)
20	3	Circle no.: yes = 1, no = 2
21, 22	3a	Enter no. of yrs.; if less than 10, enter 0 in col. 21. If item 3 is answered No. 3a is not coded.
23, 24	4	Enter no. of yrs.

Column(s)	Item No.	Code
25, 26	5	Enter no. of yrs.; if less than 10, enter 0 in col. 25.
27	6	Circle no.: married = 1, single = 2; divorced or separated = 3, widow(er) = 4
28	7	Enter no. of dependents; if more than 10, enter 9
29, 30	8c	See page(s) 133 (Refuse) or 2a (Scrap). Base code on answers to C, 8b, and/or 8c. If necessary, change response to Item C to correspond to the answer given in 8c.
31	8d	Circle no.: mainly curb = 1; mainly non-curb = 2 (item omitted in Scrap Ques.). If not a blue collar or not in collection, leave blank.
32	9	Circle no.: union = 1; non-union = 2
33	10	Circle no.: no one = 1; co-worker = 2; etc.
34	10a	Circle no.: 1 day or less = 1, 2-5 days = 2, . . .; more than 20 days = 5. If 10 is answered "No one," 10a is left blank.
35	10b	Circle no.: yes = 1; no = 2.
36	10c	Circle no.: co-worker = 1; foreman = 2; etc. If 10b is answered "no," 10c & 10d are left blank.
37	10d	Same as col. 34.
38, 39	10a+d	Enter sum of codes in cols. 34 & 37 (if less than 10, enter 0 in col. 38). (Count an "NA" or "No" response as "0" when adding.)
40	10e	Circle no.: yes = 1; no = 2.
41	10f	Same as col. 34. If 10e is answered "No", 10f is left blank.
42	11a	Enter no. of days.
43, 44	11b	Enter no. of hours; if less than 10, enter 0 in col. 43.
45, 46	11c	Same as cols. 43, 44.
47, 48	11d	Same as cols. 43, 44.

Column(s)	Item No.	Code
49, 50	11e	Round off to just two digits; if third digit is 5, round to nearest even no. (except if less than $1.00, enter 0 in col. 49 and round to 1 digit). If blank, compute using 11h and 11d.
51, 52	11f	Same as cols. 49, 50. If left blank, even though 11c was not 0, call back for verification.
53, 54	11g	Same as cols. 49, 50 (except if less than $100, enter 0 in col. 53 and round to 1 digit).
55, 56	11h	Same as cols. 53, 54.
57	12a	Circle no.: yes = 1; no = 2.
58	12b	Enter no. of promotions. If 12a is answered "NA" or "No", enter "0". <u>Do Not enter "X" or leave blank</u>, unless employee refuses to answer.
59, 60	(below 12b)	Divide no. in col. 58 by no. in cols. 17 & 18 and enter. Proportion is rounded to 1 digit (e.g., if col. 58 = 1 & cols. 17 & 18 = 10, proportion is 1/10 or .10); round to 1 and enter no.; if proportion is greater than 1, enter 9. If no promotions, enter "0".
61, 62	12c	Same as cols. 17 & 18. If no promotions made. do not code.
63	13a	Circle no.: yes = 1; no = 2.
64, 65	13b	Enter no. of raises. If 13a is answered "NA" or "No", enter "0". <u>Do Not enter "X" or leave blank</u>, unless employee refuses to answer.
66, 67	(below 13b)	Same as cols. 59, 60.
68, 69	13c	Same as cols. 61 & 62.
70-79	14a-g	For each set of three cols.: if check appears in left-hand column, circle 1, if check appears in second column, circle 2; if third column, circle 3. If interviewer neglects to check one of first three cols., then check "No" column, and circle appropriate code no. If "No" or "Don't know" in the first three columns, the second three columns are left blank. If the interviewer checks "Yes" in first column and does not check any of last 3 cols., call back.
80		Card Number 1 should already be checked

CARD 2

Column(s)	Item No.	Code
1-4	Cover	Do not code
5, 6, 7, 8	14h-k	Same as cols. 70-79 (Card 1)
9, 10	(below 14)	Compute and enter total no. of 1's circled in "Yes" col. (if less than 10, enter 0 in col. 9)
11-18	15a	Circle no.: yes = 1; no = 2. If question is marked "no promotions possible," code "No" for each alternative. if marked "NA", write and circle "X" over each code #2 ("NO" column).
19, 20	15b-c	Circle no. opposite checked alternative. If no yes's in 15a, leave 15b and 15c blank. If one yes, circle 15b code across from that alternative and leave 15c blank. If more than two alternatives are answered yes and either or both 15b and 15c is blank, call back.
21-24	16, 17a, b, c	Circle or enter no. corresponding to no. entered or checked in blank opposite. If interviewer writes "NA" because "no chances for raise or promotion," do Not enter "X", write "1" (which means "no chance" on Card A) instead.
25	19	Enter no. in blank opposite. If no answer because item 18 is answered "same as present job," code "0", otherwise, code "X".
26, 27	(20, Gross pay/wk.)	Enter last two digits (rounded as usual) of no. in parentheses (if less than $100, enter 0 in col. 21). If unknown, code "X" by each column.
28, 29, 30	21a, b, c	Same as cols. 21-24.
31	22	Circle no.: Public employment agency = 1; Private agency = 2; etc.; if other, enter and circle 8.
32	23	See page(s) 134 ; if multiple answers, call back to get most important.
33, 34	24a	Enter no. of yrs. (rounded as usual); if less than 10, enter 0 in col. 33. If do not know, enter "XX".
35	24b	Yes = 1; no = 2. If don't know/no answer, mark "X" over the 1 and circle it.
36	25	Yes = 1; no = 2. If don't know/no answer, mark "X" over the 1 and circle it.

Column(s)	Item No.	Code
37-47	26-35a, b	Enter no. in blank; if NA, do not code.
48, 49	(below 35)	Enter sum of answers to items 26 through 35b, providing there are no blank responses. If there is one or more "No" responses, see page(s) 146.
50-55	36, 37	See page(s) 136-139 (if NA, enter "X"); Cols. 50 & 51 and 53 & 54 for Event; 52 & 55 for Agent. If two events are listed, code for the one underlined or that appears to be most fundamental or important. Call back if necessary.
	(below 37)	If Q. 36 is checked, circle 1; if Q. 37, circle 2.
	38	Do not code this item.
56, 57	39, 40	Circle no. opposite checked blank.
58, 59, 60	41	See page(s) 140 (if NA, enter "X").
61-68	42, 43	See page(s) 141 (if NA or blank - leave blank. Do NOT code "X" if not answered.
	(below 43, use coding space below 37)	If Q. 42 is checked, circle 3; if Q. 43, circle 4.
69	44	Circle no.: yes = 1; no = 2.
70, 72, 74, 76, 78	45, 45b d, f, h	Enter no.: Yes with no other job listed = 1, no = 2; Yes (if other job is listed and is in solid waste field) = 3; Yes (if another job is listed and is not in solid waste field) = 4.
71, 73, 75, 77, 79	45a, c, e, g, i	See page(s) 142 (if previous item was answered "No", leave blank).
80		Card Number Circle 2

Interviewer Code

Employee Questionnaire   Cols. 5 & 6 (Refuse and 5093)

Code	Interviewer
30	Corbett
31	Jackson
32	Reed
34	Kluver
79	Klisch
80	Schocker
81	Falls
83	Ely
84	McKenzie
85	Patrick
86	Ruby
87	Nibarger
90	Gentry
91	Ramos
92	Hamilton

Cols. 7 & 8 Company Size

Code	No. of Employees	
00	1- 5	(found by determining total no. of employees in all job levels combined from the matching Management Questionnaire
01	6- 15	
02	16- 25	
03	26- 50	
04	51- 75	
05	76- 100	
06	101- 200	
07	201- 500	
08	501-1000	
09	1001-2000	

Item D	Col. 11 (refuse & 5093)
Code	Response
1	W
2	B
3	Mexican (write in code and circle)

Item 8c, Cols. 29, 30

Job Level	Code	Job Category	Job Level	Code	Job Category
Management			Skilled		
	1.	General management (including personnel, sales, and planning personnel who spend 50% of their time on solid waste)		15.	Maintenance
				16.	Collection & transport driver
				17.	Transfer trailer driver
	2.	Regulatory		18.	Weighmaster
	3.	Scientific, research, technical, accounting, etc.		19.	Crane loader or bulldozer operator
	4.	Other		20.	Furnace operator (stoker)
Secretarial				21.	Incinerator, residue removal
	5.	Clerical (or bookkeeper)		22.	Other
	6.	Secretarial	Unskilled		
	7.	Dispathers		23.	Collection and transportation helper
	8.	Other			
Supervisory				24.	Sanitary landfill
	9.	Collection & transportation		25.	Incinerator helper
	10.	Sanitary landfill		26.	Open-dump helper
	11.	Incineratory			
	12.	Open dump		27.	Recycling and recovery helper
	13.	Recycling & recovery		28.	Other
	14.	Other			

Item 23, Col. 32

Code	Response
0	<u>Pay/benefits/job security</u>
1	Needed a job (was laid off previous); job available; no other available; Co. needed someone
2	<u>Relative(s) or friend(s)</u> in field or in Co.; like specific people in Co.; knew someone personally
3	Liked <u>type of work</u>; challenge of work; interest in work or equipment; done it before; different work
4	<u>Working conditions</u>: hours; location (outside, close to home), etc.
5	<u>Chance(s) for advancement</u> (no chance in previous job)
6	Type of <u>Supervision</u> (e.g., freedom from supervision)
7	Assigned to the job under civil service system
y	Chance; circumstance; no reason

If there is a blank or "NA" response to Items 26-35a, b, compute the sums as follows:

Find the median answer* to the other items (e.g.,; "4") and use this no. in place of the blank in computing the total; then enter total. (Do not use this median no. in coding the single item; the item is not coded.) If there is more than one non-coded item in Items 26-35a, b, leave Cols. 48 and 49 blank

---

*The median is the answer (number) which is greater and smaller than half the responses. Thus, if responses were: 7, 7, 6, 6, 6, 4, 3, 3, 3, 2, 2, median would be 4 because there are 5 bigger and 5 smaller nos. If median does not fall exactly on a no., use nearest whole number or decide by a coin toss between the two closest numbers.

Coding categories to be used for Items 36 and 37. Cols. 50 & 51, and 53 & 54, should be used for Event code (put 0 in 1st col. if code no. is less than 10); Cols. 52 & 55 are for Agent code.

GOOD DAY EVENT CATEGORIES

01. Task Activity: enjoyed the work task or task activity itself (regardless of external rewards or outcomes). Given a desired task assignment. Saw the work as important, significant, or meaningful.

02. Amount of Work: amount of work just right; neither too much nor too little; work was easy to do or light (no specific success involved).

03. Smoothness: work went smoothly without (temporary) distraction or interruption; work done efficiently (but no specific success involved).

04. Success (work achievement in relation to some standard): finished a task; completed an assignment or project; solved a problem; reached a work goal; met a deadline; did a job especially well or fast or skillfully; improved performance; had a project or solution accepted by others; saw ultimate success of work; getting a contract (if success was most salient); reaching a sales figure if it represents a standard of achievement. Successfully learned a new skill or mastered a new task.

05. Promotion: to a higher position; promise of promotion.

06. Responsibility: was increased, given special assignment (not necessarily promoted).

07. Verbal (or implied Verbal) Recognition for Work: praised, thanked, complimented, given credit, given award, or special recognition for a piece of work or for performance in general (by company, supervisor, co-workers, subordinates, customers, etc.); given high rating for work; no complaints.

08. Money: received a monetary raise or bonus or tip; made a profit; got money for overtime work; promise of a raise; getting a contract (if money was most salient; see also #4). Good or high benefits. Job security.

09. Interpersonal Atmosphere in general was pleasant; everyone was getting along well together, polite, friendly, interesting conversations; pleasant non-work interaction with others (e.g., office party); praised for non-work action. (Note: do not use this if praise was for work; see #7).

10. Physical Working Conditions pleasant: weather, temperature, humidity; air; machinery; hours of work (e.g., short hours, good shift, free time, good lunch breaks, rest periods); location; physical surroundings of work; etc.

11. Uncodable or Other: e.g., outcome of union election, family event, etc.

BAD DAY EVENT CATEGORIES

01. Task Activity: did not enjoy or disliked the work or task activity itself (regardless of external rewards or outcomes). Given a disliked or undesired task assignment (e.g., a dirty job). Saw the work as unimportant, insignificant, or meaningless.

02. Amount of Work: not reasonable, too much or too little; work was especially heavy or hard or difficult (no specific failure involved).

03. Smoothness: work did not go smoothly. Temporary interruptions, delays or distractions; wasted time; work done inefficiently. (Note: if actual failure, use #4 below). Accident or breakdown if this caused lack of smoothness.

04. Failure (work failure in relation to some standard): did not finish a task; did not complete an assignment or project; did not solve a problem; failed to reach a work goal; did not make a deadline; did a job especially poorly or slowly or unskillfully; failed to improve performance or did worse than before; had a project or solution rejected by others; saw ultimate "failure" of work because not used or results of work damaged or destroyed; failed to get contract or reach sales figure (if failure was most salient); caused an accident (if seen as failure). Failed to learn a new skill or successfully master a new task.

05. Demotion or Lack of Promotion: did not get a desired promotion or promised promotion; no opportunity for promotion (blocked opportunity).

06. Responsibility was not increased as desired or as promised; did not get special assignment that wanted to get; too much/too little responsibility; given responsibility without adequate training; reduction of responsibility.

07. Negative Verbal (or implied Verbal) Recognition (or Lack of Recognition) For Work: criticized, blamed, not thanked, not complimented, not given credit or credit stolen by another, not given award, given reprimand, insulted for a piece of work or for performance in general (by company, supervisor, co-workers, subordinates, customers); false accusation; given low rating for work; gesture or look of disapproval; complaint about product or work.

08. Money: did not receive a desired raise or promised money bonus; did not make a profit; no overtime pay; no tip or low tip; salary or raise unfair (compared to others); failed to get contract or sale (if money was most salient; see also #4). Low or lack of sufficient benefits.

09. Interpersonal Atmosphere: in general, was unpleasant, everyone was getting along poorly, hostile, unfriendly, touchy, etc.; obscene language used in presence; dull conversation; unpleasant non-work interaction with others; criticized for non-work action. (Note: do not use this if criticized for work, see #7.)

BAD DAY EVENT CATEGORIES (CONT.)

10. <u>Physical Working Conditions</u> unpleasant: weather, temperature, humidity; air; machinery; hours of work (e.g., long or late hours, bad shift, no free time, short lunch breaks, no rest periods, etc.); location; failure to get desired time off; physical surroundings of work; etc.

11. <u>Uncodable or other</u>; e.g., outcome of union election, accident (that does not belong in #4 above), strike, family problem, etc.

GOOD AND BAD DAY AGENT CATEGORIES

1. <u>Self</u> (the respondent himself).

2. <u>Supervisor</u> or other specific superior or superiors of respondent.

3. <u>Co-worker(s)</u> of respondent (someone at same level in organization or profession).

4. <u>Subordinates(s)</u> of respondent (someone at lower level in organization or profession).

5. <u>Organizations</u>, management or organizational policies. (No particular person or persons cited).

6. <u>Customer</u> of respondent (including students, patients, buyers, etc.).

7. <u>Non-human agent</u> (nature, machinery, weather, neighborhood, equipment, "God", etc.).

8. <u>No agent</u> indicated (e.g., luck, the "breaks," "that's the way it is") or "do not know", or unclassifiable.

9. <u>Union</u>.

Item 41, Cols. 58, 59, 60

Col. 58:	Code	Mood
	0	Negative, bad, unpleasant, anxious, worried, tense
	1	Neutral, nothing, no feeling, do not care
	2	Positive, good, pleasant, looking forward, happy, proud, ready to go

Cols. 59 60	Code	Content of Thought
	00	None, blank, no thought of job, do job mechanically
	01	Being on time, getting to work OK--or on time
	02	Work to be done (tasks, responsibilities, getting out the trucks, smell of work, work going smoothly, getting work done right or well, etc.)
	03	Amount or heaviness or difficulty of work; amount of business; hardness or easiness of day's work
	04	Quitting job; quitting time; getting done on time or early (getting it over with)
	05	Working conditions: weather, location, hours, etc.
	06	Subordinates: would they show up; ability to do job; who to use; subordinates' past performance
	07	Supervision/Management: disorganization of work, relations with supervisor or management
	08	Avoiding relief: supporting family, pay
	09	Off-the-job activities
	0x	No answer
	0y	Uncodable

Items 42, 43, Cols. 61-68

Code	Response
00	**Work itself:** responsibility, boredom, variety, trading off, smell, dirtiness, importance of work
01	**Success, failure,** accomplishment, pride, doing job well, finish on time, doing good work, knowing job well, challenge of job
02	**Smoothness** of **own** work (caused by breakdowns, slowness of others, incompetence, or the opposite) (see also #y)
03	**Amount, difficulty, or heaviness** of work (curb service?); amount of trash, amount of business, getting done
04	**Promotion:** chances for, training programs to help advancement
05	**Pay** (payday)/Benefits (bonuses)/**Security** (steadiness)
06	**Supervision/Management:** good, poor, limited, helpful, not helpful, considerate, etc.; poor communication, qualifications of, attitudes of
07	**Co-workers:** amount of work, competence, cooperation
08	**Subordinates:** absenteeism, turnover, attitudes, following orders, competence, incompetence, adequacy, etc.
09	**Customers:** complaints; compliments, satisfaction
0x	**Working conditions:** hours, rest, lunch, weekend and holiday work, earliness, lateness, time off, weather, location, service building
0y	**Equipment:** good, poor, need repairs, breakdown, etc. (see also #2)

(Items 45a, c, e, g, i)

Code	Response
0	No opening now (layoffs)
1	Pay/Benefits
2	Security/Seniority
3	Union membership or politics
4	Work itself (better here than other job) more respectable, interesting
5	Working conditions: hours, need to move or travel, weather
6	Age
7	Obligation to present employer (needed here)
8	Management/Supervisors/Co-workers (don't like, like, did not or do get along with, etc.
x	No answer
y	Nothing is stopping me, plan to change job soon

CARD A

EMPLOYEE QUESTIONNAIRE

__1__ no chance at all

__2__ slight chance

__3__ moderate (50-50) chance

__4__ good chance

__5__ almost certain chance

CARD B

EMPLOYEE QUESTIONNAIRE

Extremely Satisfied	Moderately Satisfied	Slightly Satisfied	Neither Satisfied nor Dissatisfied	Slightly Dissatisfied	Moderately Dissatisfied	Extremely Dissatisfied
7	6	5	4	3	2	1

CARD C

EMPLOYEE QUESTIONNAIRE

 1 definitely would not
 2 probably would not
 3 might or might not
 4 probably would
 5 definitely would

SELECTED BIBLIOGRAPHY

Acton Society Trust, Size and Morale, Part I (London 1953), Part II (London 1953).

Alderfer, C.P., "An Empirical Test of a New Theory of Human Needs", Organizational Behavior and Human Performance, Volume 4, 1969.

Alderfer, C.P., "Job Enlargement and Organizational Context", Personnel Psychology, Volume 22, 1969.

Argyle, M., "Supervisory Methods Related to Productivity, Absenteeism, and Labor Turnover", Human Relations, Volume II, 1958.

Bachman, J.G., Smith, G.C., and Slesinger, J.A., "Control, Performance, and Satisfaction; An Analysis of Structural and Individual Effects", Journal of Personality and Social Psychology, Volume 4, 1966.

Baumgartel, H., and Sobol, R., "Background and Organizational Factors in Absenteeism", Personnel Psychology, Volume 12, 1959.

Beer, M., "Organizational Size and Job Satisfaction", Academy of Management Journal, Volume 7, 1964.

Bishop, R.C., and Hill, J.W., "Effects of Job Enlargement and Job Changes on Contiguous But Nonmanipulated Jobs as a Function of Workers Status", Journal of Applied Psychology, Volume 55, 1971.

Bowen, D., and Siegel, P., "Relationship Between Satisfaction and Performance: Question of Causality", Proceedings, 78th Annual Convention, American Psychological Association, 1970.

Brayfield, A.H., and Crockett, W.H., "Employee Attitudes and Employee Performance", Psychological Bulletin, 1955.

Caplow, T., "Organization Size", Administrative Science Quarterly, Volume 1, 1957.

Centers, R., and Bugental, D., "Intrinsic and Extrinsic Job Motivations Among Different Segments of the Working Population", Journal of Applied Psychology, Volume 50, 1966.

Cleland, S., The Influence of Plant Size on Industrial Relations, Princeton, 1955.

Cummings, L.L., Schwab, D.P., and Rosen, M., "Performance and Knowledge of Results as Determinants of Goal Setting", Journal of Applied Psychology, 1971.

Durkheim, E., The Division of Labor in Society, Glencoe, Ill., 1953.

Farris, G.F., "A Predictive Study of Turnover", Personnel Psychology, Volume 24, 1971.

Filley, A.C., "A Theory of Small Business and Divisional Growth", Unpublished Ph.D. Dissertation, Department of Business Organization, Ohio State University, 1961.

Filley, A.C , and House, R.J., Managerial Process and Organizational Behavior, Glenview: Scott, Foresman, 1969.

Fisher, P.H., "An Analysis of the Primary Work Group", Sociometry, Volume 16, 1953.

Ford, R.N., Motivation Through the Work Itself, New York: American Management Association, 1969.

French, J.R.P., and Raven, B., "The Bases of Social Power", D. Cartwright (Ed.), Studies in Social Power, Ann Arbor, University of Michigan, 1959.

General Electric Company Behavioral Research Service, "Attitudes Associated with Turnover of Highly Regarded Employees", Crotonville, New York: Author, 1964(a).

General Electric Company, Behavioral Research Service, "A Comparison of Work Planning Program with the Annual Performance Appraisal Interview Approach", Crotonville, New York: Author 1964(b).

Goldthorpe, J.H., "Orientation to Work and Industrial Behavior: A Contribution to the Acton Approach in Industrial Sociology", Unpublished Paper, Cambridge, 1964.

Goldthorpe, J.H., "Social Stratification and Industrial Society", in Paul Halmos (Ed.), The Development of Industrial Society, Sociological Review Monograph, 1964.

Goldthorpe, J.H., "Attitudes and Behavior of Car Assembly Workers: A Deviant Case and Theoretical Critique", British Journal of Sociology, Volume 17, 1966.

Goldthorpe, J.H., Lockwood, D., Bechhofer, F., and Platt, J., The Affluent Worker: Industrial Attitudes and Behavior, Cambridge, 1968.

Golembiewski, R.T., Men, Management, and Morality, New York, McGraw-Hill, 1965.

Gouldner, A.W., Patterns of Industrial Bureaucracy, London, 1955.

Guest, R.H., "A Neglected Factor in Labour Turnover", Occupational Psychology, Volume 29, 1955.

Hackman, J.R., and Lawler, E.E., III, "Employee Reactions to Job Characteristics", Journal of Applied Psychology, Volume 55, 1971.

Haire, M.E., Ghiselli, E., and Porter, L.W., Managerial Thinking: An International Study, New York: Wiley, 1966.

Hall, R.F., Haas, J.E., Johnson, N.H., "Organization Size, Complexity, and Formalization", American Sociological Review, Volume 32, 1967.

Hare, A.P., "Interaction and Consensus in Different Sized Groups", American Sociological Review, Volume 17, 1952.

Hellriegel, D., and Slocum, J.W., Management: A Contingency Approach, Addison-Wesley, 1974.

Herbst, P.G., "The Measurement of Behavioral Structures by Means of Input-Output Data", Human Relations, Volume 10, 1957.

Herzberg, F., Mausner, B., Peterson, R.O., and Capwell, D.F., Job Attitudes: Review of Research and Opinion, Pittsburgh: Psychological Service of Pittsburgh, 1957.

Hewitt, D., Parfit, J., "A Note on Working Morale and Size of Group", Occupational Psychology, Volume 27, 1953.

Hickson, D.J., Pugh, D.S., and Pheysey, D.C., "Operations Technology and Organization Structure: An Empirical Reappraisal", Administrative Science Quarterly, Volume 14, 1969.

Hinrichs, J.R., "Psychology of Men at Work", Annual Review of Psychology, 1970.

Holden, P.E., Pederson, C.A., and Germane, G.E., Top Management, New York: McGraw-Hill, 1968.

House, R.J., and Miner, J.B., "Merging Management and Behavioral Theory: The Interaction Between Span of Control and Group Size", Administrative Science Quarterly, Volume 14, 1969.

Hulin, C.L., "Job Satisfaction and Turnover in a Female Clerical Population", Journal of Applied Psychology, 1966.

Hulin, C.L., "Effects of Changes in Job Satisfaction Levels in Employee Turnover", Journal of Applied Psychology, 1968.

Hulin, C.L., and Blood, M.R., "Job Enlargement, Individual Differences, and Worker Responses", Psychological Bulletin, Volume 60, 1968.

Indik, B.P., "Organization Size and Member Participation: Some Empirical Tests of Alternative Explanations", Human Relations, Volume 18, 1965.

Indik, B.P., "Some Effects of Organization Size on Member Attitudes and Behavior", Human Relations, Volume 16, 1963.

Ingham, G.K., "Organization Size, Orientation to Work and Industrial Behaviour", Sociology, Volume 1, 1967.

Ingham, G.K., Size of Industrial Organization and Worker Behaviour, Cambridge University Press, 1970.

Katzell, M.E., "Expectations and Dropouts in Schools of Nursing", Journal of Applied Psychology, Volume 52, 1968.

Kerr, W.A., "Labor Turnover and Its Correlates", Journal of Applied Psychology, Volume 31, 1949.

Kerr, W., Koppelmeier, G., and Sullivan, J., "Absenteeism, Turnover, and Morale in a Metals Fabrication Factory", Occupational Psychology, 1951.

Killbridge, M., "Turnover, Absence, and Transfer Rates as Indicators of Employee Dissatisfaction with Repetitive Work", Industrial and Labor Relations Review, Volume 15, 1961.

Kornhauser, A., Mental Health of the Industrial Worker, New York: John Wiley, 1965.

Lawler, E.E., "Job Attitudes and Employee Motivation: Theory, Research, and Practice", Personnel Psychology, 1970.

Lefkowitz, J., and Katz, M., "Validity of Exit Interviews", Personnel Psychology, Volume 22, 1969.

Locke, E.A., "Job Satisfaction and Job Performance: A Theoretical Analysis", Organizational Behavior and Human Performance, Volume 5, 1970.

Locke, E.A., "Toward A Theory of Task Motivation and Incentives", Organizational Behavior and Human Performance, Volume 3, 1968.

Locke, E.A., "What Is Job Satisfaction?", Organizational Behavior and Human Performance, Volume 4, 1969.

Locke, E.A., Bryan, J.F., and Kendall, L.M., "Goals and Intentions as Mediators of the Effects of Monetary Incentives on Behavior", Journal of Applied Psychology, Volume 52, 1968.

Macedonia, R.M., "Expectation-Press and Survival", Unpublished Doctoral Dissertation, Graduate School of Public Administration, New York University, June 1969.

Mandell, M., Recruiting and Selecting Office Employees, New York: American Management Association, 1956.

Marriott, R., "Size of Work Group and Output", Occupational Psychology, Volume 26, 1949.

Mayo, E., and Lombard, G.F.F., "Team Work and Labor Turnover in the Aircraft Industry of Southern California", Graduate School of Business, Harvard University Publications, Number 32, 1944.

Metzner, H., and Mann, F., "Employee Attitudes and Absences", Personnel Psychology, Volume 6, 1953.

Mikes, P.S., and Hulin, C., "Use of Importance as a Weighting Component of Job Satisfaction", Journal of Applied Psychology, 1968.

Miner, J.B., "Bridging the Gulf in Organizational Performance", Harvard Business Review, Volume 46, 1968.

Miner, J.B., The Management Process, New York: Macmillan, 1973.

Miner, J.B., and Miner, M.G., Personnel and Industrial Relations, Macmillan, 1973.

Poidevin, S.L., "A Study of Factors Affecting Labor Turnover", Personnel Practice Bulletin, Volume 1, 1949.

Porter, L.W., "Where Is the Organization Man?", Harvard Business Review, Volume 41, 1963.

Porter, L.W., and Lawler, E.E., "Properties of Organization Structure in Relation to Job Attitudes and Job Behavior", Psychological Bulletin, Volume 64, 1965.

Porter, L.W., and Lawler, E.E., "The Effects of Tall Versus Flat Organization Structures on Managerial Job Satisfaction", Personnel Psychology, Volume 17, 1964.

Porter, L.W., and Mitchell, V.F., "Business Hierarchies", Journal of Applied Psychology, Volume 51, 1967.

Porter, L.W., and Steers, R.M., "Organizational, Work, and Personal Factors in Employee Turnover and Absenteeism", Psychological Bulletin, Volume 80, 1973.

Revans, R.W., "Human Relations, Management, and Size", In E.M. Hugh-Jones (Ed.), Human Relations and Modern Management, Amsterdam: North Holland Publishing, 1958.

Revans, R.W., "Industrial Morale and Size of Unit", Political Quarterly, Volume 27, 1956.

Rhinehart, J.B., Bassell, R.P., DeWolfe, A.S., Griffin, J.E., and Spaner, F.E., "Comparative Study of Need Satisfactions in Governmental and Business Hierarchies", Journal of Applied Psychology, Volume 3, 1969.

Schuster, J.R., Collette, J.A., and Knowles, L., "The Relationship Between Perceptions Concerning Magnitudes of Pay and the Perceived Utility of Pay: Public and Private Organizations Compared", Organizational Behavior and Human Performance, Volume 9, number 1, February 1973.

Sexton, W.P., "Organizational and Industrial Needs: A Conflict?", Personnel Journal, Volume 46, 1967.

Slater, P.E., "Contrasting Correlates of Group Size", Sociometry, Volume 21, 1958.

Stekler, H., Profitability and Size of Firm, Berkeley Press, 1968.

Talacchi, S., "Organizational Size, Individual Attitudes, and Behavior: An Empirical Study", Administrative Science Quarterly, Volume 5, 1960.

Taylor, K.E., and Weiss, D.J., "Prediction of Individual Job Turnover From Measured Job Satisfaction", Proceeding of 77th Annual Convention of the American Psychological Association, 1969.

Telly, C.S., French, W.L., and Scott, W.G., "The Relationship of Inequity to Turnover Among Hourly Workers", Administrative Science Quarterly, Volume 16, 1971.

Terrien, F., and Mills, D., "The Effect of Changing Size Upon the Internal Structure of Organizations", American Sociological Review, Volume 20, 1955.

Thomas, E.J., and Fink, C.F., "Effects of Group Size", Psychological Bulletin, Volume 60, 1963.

Turner, A.N., and Lawrence, P.R., "Industrial Jobs and the Worker: An Investigation of Responses to Task Attributes", Boston: Harvard University Press, Division of Research, 1965.

Viteles, M.S., "The Two Faces of Applied Psychology", International Review of Applied Psychology, 1969.

Vroom, V., Work and Motivation, New York: Wiley, 1964.

Walker, C.R., and Guest, R.H., The Man on the Assembly Line, Cambridge: Harvard University Press, 1952.

Waters, L.K., and Roach, D., "The Relationship Between Job Attitudes and Two Forms of Withdrawal From the Work Situation", Journal of Applied Psychology, Volume 55, 1971.

Weber, M., The Theory of Social and Economic Organization New York: The Free Press, 1947.

Weissenberg, P., and Gruenfeld, L., "Relationship Between Job Satisfaction and Job Involvement", Journal of Applied Psychology, Volume 52, 1968.

Weitz, J., and Nuckols, R.C., "Job Satisfaction and Job Survival", Journal of Applied Psychology, 1955.

Wild, R., "Job Needs, Job Satisfaction, and Job Behavior of Women Manual Workers", Journal of Applied Psychology, 1970.

Wofford, J.C., "The Motivational Bases of Job Satisfaction and Job Performance", Personnel Psychology, Volume 24, 1971.

Worthy, James, "Organizational Structure and Employee Morale", American Sociological Review, 1950.

Zurcher, L.A., Meadow, A., and Zurcher, S.L., "Value Orientation, Role Conflict, and Alienation from Work: A Cross Cultural Study", American Sociological Review, Volume 30, 1965.

Authors Index

Acton Society Trust 44, 47
Alderfer, C. P. 46
Argyle, M. 16, 41

Bachman, J. G. 15, 39, 99
Bassell, R. P. 42
Baumgartel, H. 44, 47
Bechhofer, F. 40, 45, 46
Beer, M. 15, 40, 42

Bishop, R. C. 46
Blood, M. R. 46
Bowen, D. 41

Brayfield, A. H. 43
Bryan, J. F. 46
Caplow, T. 15, 16, 60
Capwell, D. F. 43

Cleland, S. 15, 16, 40
Collette, J. A. 46
Crockett, W. H. 43
DeWolfe, A. S. 42
Durkheim, E. 98

Farris, G. F. 45

Filley, A. C. 15, 39, 41, 60
Fink, C. F. 42, 44, 48
Fisher, P. H. 40, 44

Ford, R. N. 43

French, J. R. P. 39
French, W. L. 45
General Electric Company Behavioral Research Service 44
Griffin, J. E. 42
Goldthorpe, J. H. 16, 40, 45, 46, 60

Golembiewski, R. T 46

Gouldner, A. W. 40
Haas, J. E. 15, 98
Hackman, J. R. 15, 45, 46

Hall, R. F. 15, 98

Hellriegel, D. 39, 40, 99

Herbst, P. G. 41

Herzberg, F. 43

Hewitt, D. 16, 42, 44, 47, 98

Hill, J. W. 46
Hinricks, J. R. 42

House, R. J. 15, 39, 40, 60

Hulin, C. L. 43, 46

Indik, B. P. 40, 44, 98

Ingham, G. K. 15, 16, 39, 45, 46, 47, 60, 98, 99
Johnson, N. H. 15, 98
Katzell, M. E. 15, 45
Kendall, L. M 46
Kerr, W. A. 43, 47

Killbridge, M. 46, 47
Knowles, L. 46
Koppelmeier, G. 43, 47
Kornhauser, A. 42

Lawler, E. E. 15, 41, 42, 43, 44, 45, 46
Lawrence, P. R. 45, 46

Locke, E. A. 41, 42, 45, 46
Lockwood, D. 40, 45, 46
Lombard, G. F. 40, 44
Macedonia, R. M. 15, 47

Mann, F. 44, 47
Marriott, R. 15, 40, 41
Mausner, B. 43
Meadows, A. 99
Metzner, H. 44, 47

Mikes, P. S. 43
Mills, D. 42, 98
Miner, J. B. 39, 40, 41, 45, 46
Miner, M. G. 41
Mitchell, V. F. 42
Nuckols, R. C. 43
Parfit, J. 16, 42, 44, 47, 98
Peterson, R. D. 43
Platt, J. 40, 45, 46
Poidevin, S. L. 43, 99

Porter, L. W. 39, 41, 42, 43, 44, 45
Raven, B. 39

Revans, R. W. 40, 41

Rinehart, J. B. 42
Roach, D. 43, 44, 45
Schuster, J. R. 46
Scott, W. G. 45
Sexton. W. P. 47
Slater, P. E. 16
Slesinger, J. A. 15, 39, 99
Slocum, J. W. 39, 40, 99
Siegel, P. 41
Smith, G. C. 15, 39, 99
Sobol, R. 44, 47
Spaner, F. E. 42
Steers, R. M. 39, 43, 45
Stekler, H. 40, 41
Sullivan, J. 43, 47
Talacchi, S. 16, 42, 44, 47, 98

Taylor, K. E. 43, 45

Telly, C. S. 45

Terrien, F. 42, 98

Thomas, G. J. 42, 44, 98

Turner, A. N. 45, 46

Viteles, M. S. 42

Vroom, V. 43

Waters, L. K. 43, 44, 45

Weber, M. 39, 98

Weiss, D. J. 43, 45

Weity, J. 43

Wild, R. 43

Wofford, J. C. 45, 46

Worthy, J. 15, 39, 41, 42, 60

Zurcher, L. A. 99

Zurcher, S. L. 99